PONNAMAL: HER STORY

By

AMY WILSON-CARMICHAEL

AUTHOR OF
'WALKER OF TINNEVELLY,'
'THINGS AS THEY ARE,' 'OVERWEIGHTS OF JOY,'
'LOTUS BUDS,'

WITH FOREWORD BY
THE RIGHT REV. HANDLEY MOULE,
BISHOP OF DURHAM

For hundreds of other excellent titles see:

www.**Classic**_Christian_**Ebooks**.com

Inspiring and uplifting classics from authors such as:

E. M. Bounds
Alfred Edersheim
Jonathan Edwards
Charles Finney
D. L. Moody
G. Campbell Morgan
Andrew Murray
George Muller
Charles Spurgeon
Hudson Taylor
R. A. Torrey
John Wesley

…and many more!

A Division of:
DREAM Publishing International

Ponnamal (on the right)

TABLE OF CONTENTS

To
DOHNAVUR

FOREWORD TO THE FIRST EDITION

BY THE BISHOP OF DURHAM

I have just completed the perusal of the proof-sheets of 'PONNAMAL.' What shall I say to commend the book to others? Simply this: Read it, and give God thanks for it; and read it again, and often. It will be a friend and helper to your faith, a kindling fire to your missionary thoughts, prayers, and efforts, a window through which you will see 'the real India' as it is not often seen, and a picture, wonderful and beautiful, of the life of the Lord lived in His missionary servants, and in the Indian sisters whom they have brought into His all-loving power and keeping.

The interests of the book are manifold. To those who know the writer's *Lotus Buds* it will be very moving to see, as it were from within, something of the most pathetic and noble rescue-work in the world. A hundred details of missionary life will assume a new reality and vividness. And, above all, the MASTER of the field, of the labourers, of the harvest, will be 'glorified in His saint,' this dear saint with the 'steadfast eyes and the brow of peace,' in whom so wonderfully, in life and in that suffering death, He showed Himself alive for evermore.

HANDLEY MOULE.

December 7, 1917.

CHAPTER 1: THE GIRL PONNAMAL

A girl stood alone in the dark, listening. No one moved about her; the old mother-in-law who slept nearby breathed steadily, she would not waken yet awhile. The girl drew back the heavy iron bolts of the door and slipped out into the night.

Out there, in the soft warm air, with the white stars looking down on her with only pity in their eyes, she stopped. She knew the thing she purposed doing was unreasonable and hopelessly wrong; but she was too desperate with loneliness to care. Life since her husband had died had been too hard to live. A widow's life in India—God only knows how hard it can be made—she could bear it no longer; she had crept out now to end it, as so many girls have ended it. The well was near; it seemed to draw her to itself. And yet she waited; and the quiet stars soothed her, and the soft night airs did their healing work.

Then as she stood came the memory of something she had read about an Indian widow in Western India who was working a great work for her country. A widow, and yet of use to India: the thing had been; could be, perhaps, again. Perhaps there was something left for her to do. She would not end all hope of it tonight.

So she stole back again and lay down on her mat, and clasped closer the little child, her only child, whom she had all but left for ever in her mad misery, and lying with unsleeping eyes thought many thoughts till dawn.

This was Ponnamal: and thus was the awakening of a spirit that was to travel far in the fields of joyful adventure.

She was born in August, 1875, that great year for India when Edward, Prince of Wales, came and stayed in simple fashion with the Collector of the district in which her home lay, and stood to be gazed at by crowds of gratified Christians at the railway-station.

And because she was born in so great a year, the village folk told her father she would be great among women. He, good man, believed them, and received her with much joy, and called her Ponnamal, which means gold.

She grew to be an attractive little maid, of a soft clear colour quite unlike the 'black' of English imagination. And quiet eyes she had that looked steadfastly out on the world; and hair that waved and curled; and delicate little hands that no work ever spoiled. The mother, a saint of typical Indian type, brought her up carefully; and when she went to school, and returned praised by all and very wise, the father felt she had indeed begun her life in an auspicious year.

At nineteen they married her, as the custom was, and too often is, with little knowledge of the one to whom they committed so dear a treasure; he was a professor in a mission college, had good pay, was of the right degree of relationship, and of course of the exact shade of suitable caste. And clothed in silken garments, and decked with pretty chains and bangles, as sweet and true as she was good to look upon, she left her father's house, girl of high spirit, but gentle as a fawn.

Of her one year of married life Ponnamal never cared to speak: it was disillusionment. Perhaps this was inevitable, for she was by nature spiritual, and he was of the earth earthy, and his pursuits apart from his college duties were not of an elevated character. She had no sort of kinship with him till her baby came, when, the Tamil being an affectionate parent, they met for the first time on common ground; and with the Indian woman's gracious gift of making the most out of little, she contented herself and was happy.

Then suddenly her husband died, and she was that most desolate of God's creatures in India, a widow.

At first the gloom was lightened by the kindness of her father "her mother having died previously", who took her home and in his simple way tried to comfort her. But even he could not quite rise above the sense of heavy disgrace and misfortune. Life seemed suddenly one long, tired perplexity.

Then pulling herself together she faced it; knew that to conquer in it she must be strong; felt that the sorrowful, considerate affection of her own people was weakening something within her. 'I wanted to learn to endure,' she told me years afterwards, 'and so I went to my father-in-law's house;' where, as all knew, she was wanted, because of the child whom the parents-in-law counted theirs, and because of some property now Ponnamal's, which they wished to appropriate. Of sympathy they knew nothing at all. Now, in real earnest, began the discipline of widowhood.

Ponnamal's mother and her mother before her had been women of that sweet and saintly type so essentially Indian, that those who know and love this land will recognize it without more descriptive words. The family had become Christian in the great-grandmother's time; and the women seem to have been notable all the way down the line, which in India, with its early marriages, covers fewer years than one might expect. The parents-in-law were also Christians of standing, but the tenderer elements somehow had been missed when they were made. Fine folk they were of their sort, people of force, some wealth, and abundant worldly wisdom. To them the girl widow was a blot on the prosperous landscape of life, to be tolerated only for the sake of the child—their son's child. With the shrewdness of a woman of this type, the mother-in-law recognized in Ponnamal something foreign in spirit and therefore obnoxious. Her harsh voice drove the girl about the house from morning till evening; and Ponnamal, who was eager to help, was treated as an unwilling drudge, to be scolded for her good. And for her good did that strange girl accept it all. The stuff which makes meek nuns scourge themselves in secret was in her. She accepted it, and at first in peace.

But little by little she sank under it. She was not allowed to keep herself nice, and that wounded the self-respect in her. Her beautiful long waves of hair might not be combed except with her fingers, and never might be dressed. Except on Sunday, when she was taken to church, she was not allowed a clean garment: soiled things become a widow. She was never allowed out anywhere except to church. In curious contradiction to this they wished Ponnamal to wear some of her jewels still, a quite unjewelled woman being too terrible a thing to have to contemplate daily. But of this Ponnamal thought little. What broke her spirit was the restricted life, the sense of being always wrong, always under the shadow of disapproval as a widow. She felt smothered. Her child, a precious little person called Paripuranam "Perfection", shortened to a purry sort of word best spelt Purripu, was hers, of course, but far more its grandmother's: so there was the constant fret of a divided responsibility and disputed claims. Sometimes she would try to lift herself above everything and triumph through sheer will-power. But will-power fails under certain forms of trial long continued. She would not give in, acknowledge herself defeated, and return to her father's house; but she slipped down. It was then the cool waters of the well in the courtyard called her. Did an angel lay his hand on her arm at that moment and draw her back? The thought that worked within her I have already told.

CHAPTER 2: ENLIGHTENED

Things were so with Ponnamal when we, Mr. and Mrs. Walker and I with them, came to live in the old mission house of Pannaivilai, less than a mile from her home. The Walkers immediately began to visit the Christian houses about us; and one day, when visiting those particular parents-in-law, they saw, standing behind a door set ajar, a girl with hair like a dark cloud falling round her face, looking out at them as they sat in a front room of the house. India is a land of mystery. We get accustomed to mysteries, and hardly think of them as mysterious. But they wondered who the wild-faced girl could be, and asked, and were told 'the widow of our son.'

And now began those wonderful days when vital religion was preached Sunday by Sunday in the village church, and the place was alive with a sense of stir and a new brightness. Among the first to be enlightened was the girl Ponnamal. She listened, one of a group of women on the right-hand side of the preacher, whose eyes, even as he poured out rapid sentences in complicated Tamil, saw everyone, took in everything. Then the Spirit who works without noise of words wrought in her, and her heart was refreshed in the multitude of peace.

From this time forward all things became different for Ponnamal. There was the same starved existence, with its cramping walls and irritating, depressing influences; and yet all things were made new. She went about her duties in a kind of triumphant serenity which not even the jarring clatter of the house could disturb. Her mother-in-law was disgusted with her; she who had devoured the life of her husband, what right had she to be happy? But there was one blessed respite, for gradually Mrs. Walker's gentleness prevailed with the old father-in-law, and he allowed Ponnamal to stay for an hour after the Sunday service and teach a class in Sunday-school. It was there I saw her first.

I can see her now, a slight figure in a dark blue sari, with a group of grown-up women round her; for the school included people of all ages, down to old grannies as ignorant as infants. Ponnamal had women who could read, so they were more or less intelligent; but what struck me was her power over them. There was something about her which was quite unusual. From that moment Ponnamal for me was a woman set apart.

But she was still held in stern bondage by the old parents-in-law, who rigidly limited the hours of her liberty. Once in an evil moment she went to a neighbour's house to comfort a poor despairing widow who had sent a message to her imploring her to come; they were very angry with her, and she was confined— coffined, I had almost written—more rigorously than ever.

But it was discipline that could not hurt her now; the sense of fret was gone. She learned fortitude, patience, and the secret of possessing that joy which is not in circumstances, and so does not depend upon them.

In those days I was immersed in the study of Tamil. But as often as I could, I went out with an Indian woman chiefly to listen and learn. Before long I had made friends with the old couple who stood like two ancient, obdurate dragons between Ponnamal and the fulness of life. I had seen the old father-in-law crush a butterfly against the church wall during a service; the action seemed symbolical of the trend of his purpose towards this, the only fragment of vivid human personality he had it in his power to crush; and oppressed by the thought of it, I tried hard to find a tender spot in the old man, and one day I found it. Before he was quite aware of it, he was solemnly assuring me that if I came on a certain afternoon which he named, Ponnamal should go out with me.

Not till sixteen years later, when Ponnamal, in the leisure of illness, was living her life over again, did I know that she counted that the day of her spiritual Jubilee, the opening of her prison door. Nor did I know of the things which kindly worked together toward pulling back the bars. For the Indian mind rarely recognizes that which ours seizes upon as the crucial thing. The real substance of a letter is scattered loose all over it, or dropped into a casual postscript, or never told at all. That which grips you in a story is there by the merest chance. And so it came to pass that not till she lay ill, and I, sitting beside her with a big volume of 'Lotus Buds' on my lap, was colouring the pictures for her, by way of drawing her into reminiscences connected therewith, did I hear the back side of that afternoon.

'After you left the house, my father-in-law repented his promise, and my mother-in-law upbraided him for making it. They decided that when you came they would say it did not happen to be convenient to allow me to go. On the afternoon appointed, they talked about the matter to some of their friends who chanced to be spending the day in the house. They said, "that *Mūsal* Missie" "they called you that because like a hare were your swift ways" "came and beguiled us into folly." And they told the foolishness into which you had caused them unawares to fall. But their friends saw the matter otherwise, and one whom they greatly respected for his age and wisdom said, "Where is the indignity? The Mūsal Missie will come in a bullock-bandy and take the girl with due respect to the place whither she wishes to go; and she will with care return her at the proper time. What indignity to your family can there be in that?" The other men all agreed, and they softened towards the proposal; and all this time I was waiting behind the door, shaking with fear lest at the last moment they would harden again.'

But when a few minutes later I arrived, all I saw was a smiling old man and a smiling old woman, and a composed, though evidently eager, girl. The eagerness, however, was well under control; there was no hint of it in the quiet manner, only it looked out of her eyes; and I saw it, and met it, and loved her.

CHAPTER 3: LOOSED

Early in June, 1897, Ponnamal, her relatives by miracle agreeing, cast in her lot with mine; and for eight years we itinerated together, with a band of women and girls who gathered round us. The people called us by a name meaning a constellation like Orion or the Pleiades, and we often got letters addressed to us under this shining name. Those years lie in memory like a handful of jewels that sparkle as I turn them over. Why do past years sparkle so? They were full of ordinary things while they were being lived; they were often dusty and dull; but they are jewels now, many-coloured, various; lighted with lights time cannot dim nor tears drown.

Outwardly our life was, I suppose, quite normal. We were an itinerating band, furnished with a flag made of folds of black, red, white, and yellow sateen, a most useful text for an impromptu sermon; and we found Eastern musical instruments useful too. Being the first women's band of its kind in the district, we walked circumspectly. I used to feel like a cat on the top of a wall, the sort of wall that is plentifully set with bits of broken bottles; for there seemed to be no end to the occasions on which 'it was necessary to be careful.' But we had excellent times notwithstanding, and our own little private springs of mirth never ran dry. Ponnamal soon recovered from the cowing effect of her parents-in-law, and proved herself a delightful companion; it was good to see the timid look passing from her, as she began to realize her liberty. And our manner of life was ideal: we had one thing to do and one only; there could be no perplexities as to which was the duty of the hour—there was only one possible duty.

Much of our time we spent in scouring the country round our different camping places. Off we would go in the early morning, walking, or by bullock-cart, as many of us as could get in, packed under its curved mat roof. Stuffiness, weariness, that appalling sensation of almost sea-sickness which never forgets to afflict those naturally inclined thereto, all these disagreeables have faded,

15

and one only remembers the loveliness of the early lights on palm, and water, and emerald sheet of rice-field; the songs by which we refreshed ourselves as we tumbled along in the heat; the pause outside the village we were to enter; the swift upward call for an open door; the entrance, all of us watching eagerly for signs of a welcome anywhere—for this was pioneer work, not work in ground prepared, and in scores of the places to which we went no white woman had ever been seen before.

Sometimes we would get out at the entrance of the village and walk on till we saw a friendly face—and we almost always found one. We usually separated then, and went two and two, and won our way past the men who would be sauntering in the front courtyard, and so penetrated to the women's rooms; or if that proved impracticable, we held an open-air meeting somewhere; or sat down wherever we could, and waited till someone came to talk, for we found—at festivals, for example—that if we waited in some quiet by-street, sitting apparently unconcerned, Indian guru-fashion, on a deserted verandah, or under a tree, that one by one people discovered us, and came and squatted down beside us and asked questions. We grew more and more to use this way of approach; it seemed to suit the temper of the people, and it led furthest in.

Then home before the heat grew too intolerable; and then after breakfast, through the hottest time, we had what would now be described as a Study Circle.

Not that we had ever heard the word, a convenient later invention; but the thing itself was our habit; and with something of the spirit with which Lady Burne-Jones tells us her husband and his friend William Morris sat down to search into the lightest word of their poet, by way of preparation for the making of the beautiful Kelmscott Press Chaucer, we, together with the other members of the women's band, turned to the well-known pages of our Classic, and searched them through and through for that without which our work would have been vain. Often Ponnamal took notes; and those notes were copied by Tamil Bible Students elsewhere, and used to reappear, to our interest and sometimes amusement, in unexpected places. In the last year of her life her comfort was for me to sit with her and read now without note or comment from that beloved Book. In this way we read the Psalms, and Gospels, and those parts of the Epistles which lead into quiet meadows, lingering over and returning again and again to the dear and long familiar words, in which she found strong consolation.

The afternoons and evenings of those years were spent much as the mornings, except that we often joined the other side of the house in its avocations, and when missions to Christians were the order of the day took our share in them. Sometimes we all went street-preaching together, with a baby organ by way of attraction; and Ponnamal, who had developed a gift of fine and forceful speech, and could hold a turbulent open-air meeting in a big busy market as easily as the decorous assembly settled in tidy rows in prayer-room or village church, was an immense help always. Coming home, especially if the afternoon had been in some irresponsive village and we were feeling low, we used to make a point of singing the happiest things we knew.

Once, for a period which seemed ages long, we were shut out of the homes of the people, because some of them had believed our report. When we went to the villages where this had happened, we were pelted with ashes and rotten garlands from the necks of the idols.

One day a great crowd drew round us, and shouted its sentiments and made a most unholy racket. We stood under a burning sun till we were too tired to stand any longer; then, as there was nothing else to be done, we knelt down in the middle of the rabble and prayed for it, after which it let us go. Once we were tom-tomed out of a village, accompanied by all the ragamuffins of the place—a new experience for Ponnamal; but she walked out of that village, I remember, with the utmost dignity, in nowise disturbed thereby. To those to whom such episodes sound rather extraordinary, and to whom the militant attitude is all wrong, I can only say that with the best intentions, as I think ours were, to live a peaceable life, we were never able to discover a way by which the captives of the devil could be delivered without offending that person. When doors lie open year after year, it only means that nothing vital has been done behind them. But open doors are such nice things that we were at first much troubled when they shut; it was then we comforted ourselves with song. And as the ultimate outcome of opposition was usually the emancipation of someone elsewhere, we learned not to be moved from our purpose by talk about the unwisdom of shutting doors.

But while we were thus shut out, it was a real trouble to us to; feel ourselves anathema; for we knew the people inside so well, and so thoroughly understood the bitterness of things to them, that we could not help sympathizing with them. 'If India were as Japan is, how different it would be!' I used to say ruefully, after a battering of spirit in some vociferous village. There they are not compelled by any idiotic social code to turn believing members out of their community, and fall upon those who only want to help them. And one day I looked at a great spider's web several feet in diameter, and saw the mighty Caste system of India. At the outer edges floated almost freely long light threads that caught the morning sun and waved responsively to the morning airs. But nearer to the centre of the web the lines were drawn close—no wandering here; and right in the heart of it crouched the creature who ruled it all. A spider in India can be quite terrific; so can that be which holds the threads of a web woven in the far beginning.

CHAPTER 4: TO WHATEVER UTMOST DISTANCE

The story this chapter tells has been told in brief elsewhere; but it is essentially Ponnamal's, and cannot be left out of this record of her life.

We had all been camping out in an interesting village, where some of the most riotous of the opposing Hindus had been converted; and we were full of happiness as we started for home. With us, in our bullock-cart, was a young wife whose husband wanted us to take her into our Starry Band for awhile, in order that she might return home able to help others. She was a silly little thing, not his equal in any way, and untouched by his ideal; but in those good days we were rich in hope, and we took her. As we rumbled along the road, the husband, who had been talking to the Walkers, who were in the bandy ahead of us, now dropped back to ours, and asked his wife to give him her jewels "the word covers all the gold and silver ornaments worn by women in South India", which he did not think became anyone who wanted to live the kind of life he desired for her. She obeyed; there was nothing in her act but just obedience, for her heart desired otherwise; but I saw an expression of intense interest in Ponnamal's face, and she told me that the evening before, while she was speaking in the open air, she had overheard a child say to her mother that when she grew up she would join that band and wear jewels 'like that sister' "herself". The words had smitten Ponnamal. She felt this was the last impression she wished to leave upon anyone's mind; she had gone to her Lord about it, and the answer that seemed to come to her was this: 'Thou shalt also be a crown of glory in the hand of the Lord, and a royal diadem in the hand of thy God.' She did not argue as to the meaning of these words. She saw in the flash of a moment herself, unjewelled, a marked woman among her own people; an eyesore, an offence. But—and the thought overwhelmed her with the joy in it—not so to the Lord her God.

When we went home she took off her jewels. How minute, how inoffensive the words appear now, set down in one short sentence! But every syllable in them burned for us then. Are your hearts set upon righteousness, O ye congregation? and do ye judge the thing that is right, O ye sons of men? The answer to that question will be given otherwise.

In South India, a woman's life down to its merest detail is governed by the law universal, called custom. Her husband, however, has power to override custom. The action therefore of the wife provoked no comment, beyond a passing wonder; besides which it was recognized by a sure instinct that the thing would not proceed far in that direction: when the time came to marry the daughters they would be suitably jewelled. Ponnamal's case was different. If she had taken off her jewels at the time of her husband's death, that would have been all right, because according to custom; but she had done this thing out of sheer love to her Lord. It broke the conventions of life: it would lead who knew how far? It was therefore unnatural, disgraceful; worse, it was pharisaical. 'Be not righteous overmuch,' was the word flung at Ponnamal.

Then what was to be, happened. A few—how few! but still to the startled and indignant eyes that watched, it was most ominous— 'inebriated with Divine love,' eager to forsake and defy the spirit of the world, stript themselves of every weight that they might the less laden run the race that lay before them; and they either returned their jewels to their families, or, if free to do so, gave them to the C.M.S. for China. One who had a long struggle with herself told me that she had never gone to sleep at night without her hand on the gold chain she wore round her neck. 'If I had loved my Saviour more, I should have loved my jewels less,' she said. The last to do this difficult thing had a hard time afterwards: she was taken from the band by her people, and suffered many things. None of us touched on the subject except when privately asked what we felt about it; but it was impossible to speak without seeming to allude to it.

How vividly, as I write, comes back to me an afternoon meeting in a church in the country. The place was full, for we were in the middle of a mission; and to the Indian Christian, meetings are a sweet delight. Before me sat rows of women, and the village being rich, their ears, cut into large loops, were laden with ornaments. But to me it had been given that day to look upon Christ Crucified. I could only speak of Calvary. Far, far from me then was any thought of the women's golden toys: all eternity was round me, and that common little building was the vestibule thereof. Then, as I spoke, I saw a woman rise. She told me afterwards that she could not bear it. Time, and the scorn of time, and its poor estimates, how trivial all appeared! 'I saw Him,' she said, 'naked of this world's glory, stript to the uttermost; and I went and made an ash-heap of my pride.'

Then the word flew round that we three, the Walkers and I, especially that I, preached heresy; and one whom we all respected, a most devout and dear Tamil fellow-worker, had an alarming dream in which he perceived me wrecking the Tamil church; and he implored Mr. Walker to allow him to deal with me. So on the floor at the entrance to the tent we, Mr. Walker, he, and I, sat for two serious hours, and he talked. We ended where we began, but we ended in affection, which was a great relief to me. Still, he was disappointed; for we could not un-see what we had seen, nor deny the change that obedience had wrought in the lives of those who had obeyed, counting it joy to have something more to offer. We left it, saying only to any who pressed us, 'If ye be otherwise minded, God, if you truly desire it, will reveal even this unto you.'

Mr. Walker's contribution to the weighty subject under dispute was characteristic. It was not in its outward form a thing that very closely touched an Englishman; but in essence it did, and he pierced through to the heart of it: 'Let's have liberty,' he said; 'people are always so anxious to circumcise Titus'—and he would not have Titus circumcised. Later, as the feeling grew more and more determined that at all costs Titus must be circumcised, he took the matter up more definitely; and as usual, careless of his own reputation for narrow-mindedness or what not, spoke out his thoughts. Liberty, like duty, was one of his golden words; and another—and it was this he championed now—was obedience.

One day, soon after the last of the band had taken off her jewels, Ponnamal's parents-in-law sent for her and said, 'Do you know what you have done? You have closed the heart of the Hindus. Till now those who according to ordinary custom would have looked coldly upon you, have received you in a remarkable manner, for to their eyes you appeared a person of consequence.' This was a new view of matters to Ponnamal, who, till she had joined the band, knew little of Hindus of the exclusive castes; however, she had an answer ready. 'I told them,' she said, 'that I thought the Holy Spirit of God was strong enough to make a way for me, even without the help of my jewels.' And to her surprise she found the difficulty did not exist. To the Hindu, what he calls piety is an attractive thing; piety includes and indeed chiefly consists in a renunciation of the good things of this life. Anything, therefore, which leans to this commends itself to him. Also, of course, an unjewelled widow was quite natural to him. So Ponnamal's undecorated person was no offence to the Hindus. 'There are no boundaries set to her devotion,' they remarked, and thought no more about it, but respected her the more.

The *furor* passed; the violence of it, so absurdly out of proportion to its importance—at least according to Western thought— diminished at length; but it left its mark. The women who had braved the storm had made a new discovery: they were no more thereafter mere biscuits in a biscuit-box, cut to correct pattern, fitted in rows, each the duplicate of the other; they had found a new thing, even their individuality; and in finding it they had gained in courage and in character. Things impossible before were now undertaken without a thought; they were free from a thousand trammels that before had entangled their feet with invisible threads. And going deeper, those who for love of the Crucified had counted all things loss and vanity, loved Him now with a new love, rejoiced with a new joy. Is there any limit to what God is prepared to do for the one who loves His Son well enough to meet His lightest wish? 'After these things'—renunciation of temporal gain—the word of the Lord came unto Abraham in a vision, saying, 'Fear not, I am thy shield and thy exceeding great reward.' After these things—not dissimilar—the word was the same.

Among Ponnamal's notebooks is one dealing with these years of camp-life; and sitting on the window-sill of the nursery yesterday, her daughter and dear little legacy to us, read to me page after page of prayers, in Ponnamal's beautiful, eager Tamil: prayers written down, as probably all true recorded prayer has ever been, for the relief of a heart too full to contain that which boiled up within it. The prayer of the time we are dealing with now touched me most: 'Thou knowest my desire: my life does not yet appear to me as thoroughly controlled by Thee. My Father, look upon the holy face of Thy Beloved, and in those of us who have thus dedicated ourselves to Thee, work so, thoroughly that to whatever utmost distance Thou canst lead us, to that utmost distance for the glory of Thy name, we shall be led by Thee.'

Looking back after fifteen years' experience of what continued to the end to be a veritable reproach, she said: 'It was to me a new emancipation. A new sense of spiritual liberty is bound up in my mind with that experience; it affected everything in such an unexpected way; it set my spirit free. I could not have done this new work "the work for the Temple children", if it had not been for the new courage that came with that break with custom, and from bondage to the fear of man.' Truly at that time Ponnamal learned to say, 'A fig for the day's smile of a worm!' or for the day's frown either; and we all went on in quietness, and let the little flies of criticism buzz as they pleased about us. 'Walk before Me and be thou perfect.' What a mercy it is that it does not say, Walk before Sarah!

It worked, too, into most convenient though lesser forms of freedom; for now the band could travel anywhere, unafraid. Night journeys along unfrequented roads had been impracticable before, and it was not always possible to travel by day. And when in after years the work for children was established, and a large company of girls, bereft of the protection the mere presence of a white man nearby affords, was left with us alone in what was then an open compound in jungle-land, the two old men of the robber caste who, according to the custom of the South, are subsidized to insure us from the attentions of that caste, came to us and said: 'We agree to continue to be your guard; but if your girls were as others are, jewelled, we would not do it—no, not for lacs of rupees.'

CHAPTER 5: UNDERLAND

We were in the midst of our usual life when the little Elf walked into it, interrupted it, and finally changed its current.

We had been for a year or so at Dohnavur, which was then Camp to us, our belongings being at Pannaivilai. It was a trial to leave Dohnavur, for there were some in the Hindu villages who were inquiring; and one in particular, who afterwards came out and was hypnotized and carried back in triumph, was much in our thoughts. But we never stayed for long anywhere in those days, being dedicated to the wanderer's calling; and Dohnavur was only one of our various headquarters while itinerating, and we had to return to Pannaivilai for another year's work on that side of the district.

Now there was in the Hindu village nearby, as I have told before, a certain child who had set her heart on escaping from the life to which her mother, hardly understanding its purport, had allowed herself to be persuaded to devote her. Her father, a man of noble character, was dead; she had escaped once and had fled to her mother, who, to the Temple woman who followed after, gave her up again. To whom then could she flee? She did not know; she only knew that one March evening, in the twilight, something within her made her run across the narrow stream that divided her village from ours, and through the wood of rustling palmyra palms, and so to the village where a great church stood, and under it she paused to wait upon events. There she was found shortly afterwards, and next morning she was brought to us. We had only arrived the day before.

Had we not arrived, what would have happened? Who can tell? We need not try to imagine. We had arrived; the woman who found the child, instead of taking her back to her people, as she told us she would have done had no one been at hand to take the responsibility of her, brought her to us; and we kept her.

25

Thereafter for awhile all went on as before; only, as evening by evening we returned from work, there was a child's loving welcome, little loving arms were round one's neck. I remember wakening up to the knowledge that there had been a very empty corner somewhere in me that the work had never filled; and I remember, too, thanking God that it was not wrong to be comforted by the love of a child.

But this is Ponnamal's story, and the Elf did not become part of that till later; so that some years must be imagined of steady work as before—on Ponnamal's part without any inkling of that to which we were being drawn; on mine, very little.

And yet underlying all our work thenceforth was a search, begun almost unconsciously, for the covered facts connected with a traffic of which now for the first time I had become thoroughly aware. The child told me many things. These things burned in me. I told them to Ponnamal. She sympathized, but did not see what we could do. Neither indeed did I. All efforts that year to save children failed. Nothing I could devise, nothing Ponnamal could do, could effect the deliverance of a single little girl.

Then the thought came to me definitely to try to find out the conditions which govern this traffic in child-life. Our constant itineration was a help in this; it brought us into contact with many people, and perpetually led to new experiences. But some of the things we did together we never talked about; for I was feeling my way in those days, and felt that talk even to those nearest me would be premature. Sometimes we drifted quietly into the midst of some big festival at night, and lost ourselves in that place about which so many who live on its edge know nothing at all. Often I used to wonder at the way it received us; and one evening the talk about me was so different from the kind everywhere reserved for people of our race, that I began to feel I had slipped unawares into something quite new. It was Alice in Wonderland over again, only it was a different wonderland. Alice in Underland would have to be its name; and was I Alice, or who? Ponnamal was herself, however, which was reassuring; and we sat and talked to the people and had some food. Presently some newcomers arrived; the place was a caravanserai, and the time was late evening. It was moonlight, and we were on the shadowy side of the wide mud verandah. As the new travellers came in and passed us, they made to me the ordinary sign of salutation to a Brahman woman, and Ponnamal beside me laughed softly; and I understood, and knew that for the first time I was inside India, the real India.

After that experience, I found it well to go there as often as possible. It was thus, while far inside this underland, deep in the recesses of some great temple court with its towering walls all round, or sitting among the friendly garland-makers as they strung jessamine and oleander into wreaths and flower-balls for the gods, I heard much unknown to me before, and gradually to me it was given to see into the heart of the matter, and to know how the laws were being evaded and the children polluted. Words fall from such discoveries: they ask for deeds, not words. But as I stood in spirit before this new knowledge, which like some great shape limb by limb took visible substance before us, I ate ashes as it were bread, and mingled my drink with weeping. Ponnamal ate of those ashes too; but that which even then was calling to me with such urgent voice that I thought those very near must hear, seemed as a vain dream to her. She would have gone with me to the mouth of hell, and did, when I had to go there; but that we should ever be able to snatch children from that open mouth was something too good to be true. We had yet to learn that nothing is too good to be true.

CHAPTER 6: THE TIME APPOINTED

It was early January, 1904, and we had now settled in Dohnavur. The Walkers were in England, and we were more occupied than ever, as their absence weighted every anxiety; for by that time many converts had come out, and whoso would know anxiety let him take charge of converts. Among the most serious of the time was the care of a lad of eighteen, who could not be sent elsewhere, and who sickened with pneumonia soon after his arrival. If he had died before his people could be summoned, there was reason to anticipate trouble; a Court case, probably, for the circumstances leaned that way. Nursing him meant sitting up at night, as there was nobody who could be depended upon to change the poultices. I left him on the morning after the crisis had been safely passed, and lay down for an hour, leaving him, as I trusted, in safe hands. Before the hour was up, a messenger came post-haste: 'He is going to die! So says the village barber. All his three pulses are talking together! He will shortly have convulsions and die.' Down I fled to the converts' quarters, found the boy had struggled out, called for the village barber, and was now fairly committed to fulfil that gentleman's predictions. He lived, remarking in English when he emerged from another crisis, 'I am too much very tired;' so that anxiety passed; only to open into another, beside which the first was as nothing.

Ponnamal meanwhile kept all going peacefully on the girls' side, and when we could we went out as before.

While things were so, unknown even to Ponnamal, who had now dropped any idea of saving the Temple children, feeling the utter hopelessness of attempts in that direction, thoughts about them were rising round me like a sea of waters that rose above my head. I could not push those thoughts away; I saw the perishing children, I heard them call. How to do anything vital I knew not; I only knew I had to try again.

Within a week I had the first Temple baby we were ever able to get. Ponnamal welcomed it; but her eyes were holden, as indeed mine were. We did not know we were on the edge of new things, and must soon stop our usual work, and, turning from the familiar ways, carve a path through the jungle, where all the way along sharp thorns would be ready to stab us as we passed—a path ending in what? New responsibilities, graver, heavier, than any we had ever undertaken. No, not ending there—ending in joy, blessed eternal overflowings, inexhaustible wells of delight.

Shortly afterwards we heard of another child. Here again it was possible to get her; she was in a Temple house, for her father had dedicated her in order to acquire merit, but the conditions were such that we were able to redeem her. This meant refunding the expenses incurred in connection with her dedication. We paid them, and she came.

Then Ponnamal was troubled. The whole thing was so new, so strange in its accompanying circumstances, that she could not feel in sympathy with it. Nor, I was sure, would the friends at home, with whom I was accustomed to talk over all new thoughts before committing them to action. And so it proved when the first letters came; for I read the doubt through all the kindness. This new adventure was assuredly to go unspeeded, and I could not wonder.

For that curious and uncomfortable faculty which not only invites but compels one to see an action from every possible point of view, and to appreciate and to sympathize in a quite uncanny fashion with what its detractors are going to say, was quick in me; I could have sat down and written the letters that were written to me by almost everyone who wrote at all. Letters which looked at things otherwise shine in my grateful memory. So I spent some days, difficult to the spirit which saw its course open before it and knew it had to travel therein, speeded or unspeeded.

But Ponnamal—I had never before for one moment been out of touch with her. I prayed for a sign from heaven to show her what had been shown to me, and it was given. Gideon's fleece we called it ever after. From that day Ponnamal never looked back. Valiant to the last, my comfort, my inspiration in darkest hours, she said as she left in what, despite the dear presence of comrades about me, felt for the moment a desolation, 'I see into the future'—and her eyes lit up with a wonderful glorious fire—'I see God with you. This work is of Him, whatever man may say. He has never failed it: He will not fail it.'

CHAPTER 7: 'WHY MENS HONOURS WOMAN?'

The following bears upon my tale, though for the moment the critical reader may doubt it. It is a cutting from the *Madras Mail*, the South Indian newspaper which we take at Dohnavur.

'Mr. R. M. D. writes to the *Times of India* as follows: "My purpos for writin on you this, is to inform your many English Brothers not to give honor and devotion to your ladys because they will in the end becum proud and then they will want vote. 2 or 3 thing happen at Victory Garden to-morrow and then I all of sudden made up my brain to write you immediate. There was many Englis womans and when mans are sitting on the bench, and womans come, man stand, and give their sit to woman. This happen 2 or 3 time to-morrow and I question you why? I again tell you why? Mans and womans are similar in this world and then why mens honours woman? If they honours old old woman, one thing, but they honours young young lady. My purpose to write this to inform the Englis Sahebloks that when they do this they spoil their feminine lady and then this lady get proud and walk like pcock and then ask vote and then spoil Ken Garden and throw bomb on Loid Gorg, put bursting powder in envelope, and post, and create other mischief. Therefore I say to my Englis, please don't spoil Englis womans in India, because by honouring them you people put in their brain the sids [seeds] of sufragetism and then they get wild like Misses Pancurs. Please please print this leter near the Ruter's Telegram with big big words."'

What the writer of this eloquent appeal to the chivalry of the Englishman would have said could he have seen Ponnamal, an Indian woman, established in charge of the Nursery at Neyoor in South Travancore, honoured exceedingly by all who came in contact with her—among others, two English doctors—imagination fails to imagine. The Princess, Mr. Walker used to call her, for she had a stately way about her with all her gentleness; and the respect he had always felt for her was not lessened when he saw her rise to this new call to the arduous. He would have 'given his sit' to such a woman ten times over, and felt honoured to do it; and yet she was just Ponnamal; and she never knew she was wonderful, and that the doctor wrote that to see her at her work was a blessing to him; and her faith, especially through dark times, was an abiding inspiration; or that when her work was finished, we should read a book and find these words descriptive of her and her common, glorious toil: 'The love of duty is the strength of heroes, and there is no way of life in which we may not set ourselves to learn that love.'

By the time the new work was well established, Mr. Walker with my mother was in Dohnavur. I do not know exactly what caused that friend of friends, Walker of Tinnevelly, to become our champion. Perhaps, as was his wont, he waited till he knew all round about a matter before committing himself; and when he knew, threw fear to the winds, and was strong. I remember the first time I was sure of his sympathy. A three-sheet official letter of criticism had come from home. I could not wonder at it. It was kind, but disapproving. To follow its counsels would have been to consign how many children? to perdition. I read it, and it chilled me, though it never occurred to me to be influenced by it. Then I went to the study where he sat writing, and gave it to him.

He read it slowly through, turning over the crackly pages with the greatest deliberation. 'There speaks the voice of ignorance,' was all he said; and I knew I could count on him thereafter. And count on him I did. For he was one of those rare valorous souls upon whom the opinion of the hour made no impression whatever. The opinion of that particular hour was summed up by a certain newspaper in India, to which, unfortunately—for it was quite out of sympathy—one of the Dohnavur books had been sent for review: we would live to repent our endeavour, was all it had to say.

A year later Mrs. Walker returned. One of the babies immediately took possession of her; loved her; said so, as only a baby can say such things. That which nothing on earth could have bought was hers the moment she entered the nursery. So she, too, was in sympathy before many days had passed.

As for my mother, she would have gathered all India into her heart; for India's imperilled children she had only one word, Welcome.

She and Ponnamal foregathered at once. My mother considered her a truly remarkable woman, and was never weary of discovering new gifts and virtues in her. Nor was I, for this new work, with its new demands upon courage and wisdom and, above all, unselfishness, found her prepared at every point. When the nursery at Neyoor had to be opened, so that some at least of the children might be within reach of medical help, it was of course Ponnamal I had asked to take charge of it. She was at that time in poor health; but Neyoor did good things for her, and she loved her nursery. The place was so beautifully kept that the doctors used to take visitors to see it; and many were the inquiries as to where she had been trained, so clever were all her devices for nursing babies, sick and well, and for managing generally. Of her own hard work few knew; it was always Ponnamal who had the illest baby by her at night; always Ponnamal who did the work which no one else had grace enough to do.

I went to Neyoor as often as I could, but it became more and more difficult to leave Dohnavur, as the family grew bigger and bigger; so that through almost all the more strenuous times Ponnamal was alone with her charge, and twice she worked through bad epidemics all but singlehanded, so far as reliable help went; handicapped by all sorts of misadventures too, but brave and resourceful as ever. One of these epidemics is indelibly marked in Arulai's memory, as she was the innocent cause of it. She had been visiting in a house in the Dohnavur village where there was small-pox, and she had not been told about it. Next week she went to Neyoor, and developed small-pox in that houseful of babies. The doctors put up a mat shelter for her some little distance from the village; and there poor Arulai and the babies, who of course followed in rapid succession, abode in what Arulai recalls as a baking oven, till they recovered, as they mercifully all did. Far otherwise was the next, when a more serious foe than small-pox attacked the little children. They died then one after the other, sometimes two in a day.

Every day through those years Ponnamal wrote to me, and every week she sent the babies' weights and notes of their progress. One of these bulletins lies before me; seventeen babies' weights are given and mother-news about each. Of the joy of the little flying visits I paid I can hardly bring myself to speak. They are too full of Ponnamal to be easy to contemplate steadily. For just that little space, a time whose minutes ran with breathless peace through the hours, she threw aside the burden of her sole responsibility, and rested her heart in me, as I rested mine in her.

Once, after a visit to the Neyoor Nursery, I asked that occasional postcards of cheer might be sent to her, knowing how she would appreciate them, especially if no address were given, as then she would not feel they must be answered, and for answers I knew she had no time. And I mentioned also babies' knitted vests, safety-pins, and soap, as things the Nursery liked. The response to this immediately was over a hundred postcards from all parts of the world, numbers of letters, safety-pins galore, and soap tucked into parcels of vests to make up weight. Ponnamal, who had no idea she was known outside the family, was amazed at this shower of pleasant things, and she stored her postcards and letters in bags and kept them to regale me when I went over. Some of them are by me now, love-words that did their work. There was one friend who always seemed to divine when trouble was within about three weeks of us, and with the trouble almost invariably would arrive a postcard with the Hampstead postmark. 'I began to look out for it when things went wrong,' Ponnamal once told me, 'and was quite surprised if it did not come.'

In a land where belief in signs and omens is cultivated as a science, it was not wonderful that the first great disaster to our work, that fatal epidemic, shook the faith of all who were not committed to it in deepest ways. Shortly after the first baptism of a group of young girls "a group unique, I suppose, in the story of missions in India" the storm fell. 'The blast of the terrible ones is as a storm against the wall' is a word which reads to us straight from life.

It is an old story now, and I would not touch on it, but for the dauntless courage it discovered in Ponnamal. Child after child died; the doctors were away, and the help at hand was hardly sufficient to deal adequately with the trouble. The two nurses—the only older ones we had—lost heart: 'If another baby dies, we shall know the blessing of God is not on this work,' was their conclusion. Another died, and another, and they prepared to depart and leave Ponnamal with the young inexperienced girls, and eight or nine babies still ill, all the sick-nursing to do, all the foods to make, and her own strength failing. Then some evil men who lived next door awoke to the opportunity; their wickedness was a nightmare to Ponnamal, with the convert girls on her hands; and I was recovering from a threatened breakdown, and till the worst was over was not allowed to go to her. From the very heart of it all she wrote "and of the evil things that befell us that year, these I have mentioned were the least", 'The storm will not last always. The waves dash into our little boat, but when the Lord says, "Peace, be still," they will lie down. Let all your prayer for us be this, that we may rest in the Will of God while the storm lasts.'

Was it wonderful that I loved her, counted her precious? 'I do not want people who come to me under certain reservations. In battle you need soldiers who fear nothing.' So said Pere Didon; so say I. Can any words fitly express the preciousness of such a one?

We had the sympathy of some in our distresses; but many seemed to agree with the nurses that these untoward happenings should be understood to imply the disapproval of Providence. Just then, when it was most needed, came a mighty cheer. It was a letter from one who understood: 'I know what you will be going through now,' she wrote, 'and how people will be telling you the attempt will end in failure, and that you are wrong to try to do the impossible; but do not heed them.' And she went on to say that she believed all work that had in it the seed of eternity was bound to pass through a baptism of suffering and be misunderstood, decried, and judged by its apparent failure or success. Let none of these things move you, was the burden of her letter; and Ponnamal rejoiced in it. 'That is the truth,' she said, 'and we shall live to prove it.'

At last the Neyoor plan grew too difficult. We had so many children that we could not manage in Dohnavur without Ponnamal. So we built another Nursery here, and on a happy day, crossed as it was by fears of all that being quite doctorless was sure to mean, but helped exceedingly by the arrival of a trained nurse, Miss Wade, henceforth a beloved co-worker, Ponnamal and her babies returned.

CHAPTER 8: CARRY ON

Dates fly from me, and I do not incline to pursue them. They do not seem to me essential to the spirit of a picture, and a picture of Ponnamal is what I want to make. But for the sake of those who esteem them and cannot be happy unless facts are fixed by these neat nails, I give forthwith those few which stand out clearest.

Between 1897 and 1905 we itinerated together. In September, 1905, Ponnamal went to take charge of the Nursery opened in Neyoor. In March, 1908, she returned to Dohnavur. On March 28, 1913, she went to hospital, struck down by cancer. From that on till August 26, 1915, she suffered.

The years that followed our gradual abandoning of the work which before had been meat and drink to us, and our equally gradual embarking upon what eventually proved to be too absorbing to leave room for anything else, do not melt, as the years before them do, in a golden haze; nor do they appear in the least as jewels pleasant to the sight. Rather are they as curtains of tapestry, with figures of glad and of sorrowful countenance worked on a background of dull drab. The canvas is rough to the touch, and I am too near the curtains to get the proper effect. I see the texture and detail, not the result. But such talk is folly. Who ever does in this life see the true result of his doing? His glooms and his glories he knows as he lives through them; sometimes the one, sometimes the other makes his day. The pattern they are weaving is hidden in confusion. And oftentime he is conscious of neither, being too tired out for any feeling but one of thankfulness for having got through. Those were the years when we seldom knew what it was to have an unbroken night's sleep, for little injured children came who needed constant care. And in the tropics it is very hard to go on without enough sleep.

What made it so difficult was that there was a constraint laid upon us to keep the work pure. In India the care of young children is not considered honourable work, and the kind of women willing to do it are not of a desirable character.

Once we were all but at the end of our strength. Shall we stop praying that children may be saved? the question almost shaped itself in that day of physical exhaustion. Prayer for helpers of the right sort had been answered by the Pastors, to whom we had sent a circular letter beseeching them to find us women of the kind we needed. 'No such women exist in the Tamil Church,' had been their calm, and as we were to prove, perfectly true reply. What were we to do? Cease to use means for the salvation of the children? Push them across the narrow space that lay between, into the arms of the Temple women, who never say, Enough? Or lower our standard and take anyone as worker who could be drawn by pay to do such work?

I can see Ponnamal now, as she stood one day wearily leaning against the nursery door, a slim, tired figure, with hands that for the moment hung limply down by her side. Then she looked up; our eyes met; each saw what the other saw, even the faces of little perishing children swept down by a black flood of waters. No, we could not slacken. But as to help?—a lower type of help would suffice for at least part of the work? We could neither of us deny that we were getting too near breaking down. We turned from the temptation, for such it was—we knew it even then to be that; and we knew it by a clearer knowledge afterwards. 'Let us work till we fall,' said Ponnamal; 'but do not let us have women in as nurses who will spoil the whole work.'

The band had scattered now, but we had a few of our own girls, converts who had been trained to honour work, and think no form of it common or unclean; and a few of the right mettle, fruit of fellow-missionaries' labours, had come in from outside. But there are close-set limits to the strength of a girl, and even when our welcome English nurse came out to our great help, the difficulty was not over, for an English woman in India cannot do all she would. Nor is it over yet; even as I write we are up against the question which yet can only admit of one answer. What shall we do? Each willing worker in the nurseries has as much as she can do. How can we go on growing? But we do go on.

One day—it feels like yesterday, but it is more than a year ago—I was much cheered by a visit from a mission school-master, who, after seeing all round the place, exclaimed: 'And I hear you are short of workers. I will dedicate my eldest daughter to this work!' I asked him if his daughter were keen to do such work, and he looked a little shy, and also I thought a little young; still, looks are deceptive, and it is never wise to press matters in the East, or to be in any sort of hurry; so I left it and felt grateful. Ponnamal was ill then, and we all saved up our cheers for her; as soon as I could I took this one to her. She was much delighted, for we welcome warmly any indication of sympathy from our Tamil friends. 'Perhaps the time will come when many will feel like that,' she remarked hopefully, and we ate our little crumb of comfort greedily. A few weeks later we heard, and it really was rather a blow, that our sympathetic friend was not yet married.

We had, while the halo of the New was still upon us, some interesting offers of service both English and Indian.

'My friend is at present connected with another missionary society, but would be pleased to join you. She is forty-five, very evangelical, and she cycles and sings.' 'It is more and more borne upon me that I am to come to you and help you in your noble work of rescuing those precious children' "or darling children, perhaps it was". 'In moments of depression I will whisper in your ear, Courage, brave heart!'—these are two of the most fondly cherished. And often even now in hours of pressure we recall the rejected offer from the very evangelical lady who cycled and sung. Would she do both at the same time and all the time, or alternately? we wonder, and we rebuke ourselves for having coldly regarded an offer to provide us with so exhilarating a spectacle, not to mention the assistance such an exhibition of cheerful agility would be in the practical work of life. And we remember too the whisper to whose tender ministry I had not inclined my ear. One day I tried its effect on Ponnamal, who was hot, and busy, and exceedingly worried over some bungling of her subordinates: 'Courage, brave heart!' She stared, too astonished for words. I am afraid that Dohnavur is not at all sentimental.

India's contributions to our necessities were oftener considered; for truly we sorely needed help, and a good, capable, middle aged pair of hands with a kind, sensible heart to direct them would have been acceptable many a time. But invariably after a few days, or, at longest, months, the owner of the hands we had so hopefully welcomed, and the heart we had imagined, discovered that it would be well 'to go and do God's work,' by which was meant become a religious instructor—the mouth in India being the member whose use brings most honour, and least of the arduous. Thus our halo faded, and we became quite commonplace, and only noted for the vice of being given to hard work, and an inconsiderate standard of truthfulness; altogether impossible people, and undesirable.

The toils of those years included for Ponnamal long journeys in the interests of children in peril. She was never robust, and the heat and racket and crush of the crowded trains, especially through night journeys, tried her very much. She would come back looking shaken to pieces, and disheartened perhaps by reason of failure; but always, when the next call came, she was ready for it. And such calls came frequently, for she was by far the most suitable for the peculiarly difficult work of child-rescue—a work which demands, and especially demanded in its early precarious days, before that invaluable thing, a precedent, was established, high courage, and wisdom. A false move then, and we should all have been plunged in tribulation; worse by far, the newly launched little boat of the new endeavour would have been wrecked on the rocks that were never very distant. A single moment's hesitation, and under certain frequent circumstances another child would have floated downstream. As it was, with all our care, we had to stand helplessly by and see many such pass us for ever.

There was one over whom she mourned with me, a little Brahman child-widow who got speech with one of us: 'Save me! I have heard of your religion, the Christian religion. They are taking me to a Temple house; I do not want to go. Save me! Make a way of escape for me that I may reach a Christian house.' She was spirited away; from town to town we traced her, then lost her in a Temple house in a South Indian city where, as one of its own Temple women told us, children are constantly adopted 'for Temple purposes.'

There was another, a charming child of seven or eight, who looked trustfully up at us and told us she was learning to dance, so that the gods might be pleased. Ponnamal dared much to save her; this work is full of the call to dare. But the child passed out of reach downstream.

And babies' faces we saw, and I see now. In the flesh I saw them first, in their white cotton hammocks, swinging in the dim low rooms of the Temple houses known to us. In the spirit I see them always on the black waters that flow without ceasing day and night through the midst of this sun-filled land. But few see them, for most eyes are full of other sights. Be it so. We may not insist upon everyone's seeing such things; but we have seen, and the effect of such seeing is to cause those who have seen to feel that no passing weariness of the flesh or spirit can ever for one moment count as against the eternal importance of getting children out of the grasp of the gods. That for us was the only thing that mattered. So we laid hold together on the word that declares that He that raised up Christ from the dead shall also quicken our mortal bodies; and we took it that if, for the right doing of the work set before us, a certain quickening was required in these our present mortal bodies, that quickening would be wrought in us by Him Who is not bound by time's to-day or to-morrow, being King of eternity. And I think it was wrought in us, or we could not have continued.

But our God was very kind to us: He sent us splendid help. I remember how Ponnamal searched the faces of the 'Sitties,' who one after another came to us through the years that followed. She was looking for that which we required—endurance, courage, a capacity for happiness, love. When she found it she was satisfied. 'God has chosen them each one,' she said to me as she lay dying;

'they will stand fast by you. I am not afraid to leave you to them; the anointing of their God is upon them.' For this work which gives so much more than anyone not in it will ever know—asks much, even all.

CHAPTER 9: 'NOUS'

Once more Walker of Tinnevelly must come into this book, for the chapter word suggests him. It was one of his favourite words. So and so 'has no *nous*' he would say in rather disgusted tones, of some hopeless muddler. Or, in tones of keen approval, 'You know where you are with him; he has plenty of *nous*.' Of Ponnamal he used to say with the particular smile that was his on such occasions, 'She's all right: she's got such *nous*, you know.' I did know it, and blessed her Creator. For *nous* appeared then to me, and has ever since appeared to be, one of the rarest of gifts, by no means to be taken for granted; and after a somewhat extended experience of a variety of types of human beings, I for one incline to put them all into one of two divisions: those who, when thrown out of a top window, fall on their feet, and those who alight otherwise. Ponnamal could be trusted to fall on her feet.

Her *nous* showed in a hundred directions.

She had a clear head for packing a day full of good honest work, and for directing the energies of others. She knew how to turn odds and ends both of time and of material to good account; and she was down to every trick of shiftiness in those about her. Slackness she abhorred; she was most un-Oriental in her attitude towards it; and she had little patience with silliness. 'You didn't know! why didn't you know?' she would demand if excessively tried; and she found *nous*-less people, however virtuous, wearisome.

It was one of Ponnamal's ways—due, I suppose, to the *nous* in her—that caused her to work at a given plan until she had got it as near perfection as possible. Take the house-keeping plan, for example. It is not easy for a reader accustomed to the convenience of civilization to conceive what it means to feed a large company of children, and workers, and frequently Indian guests, in a jungle place, far from shops and markets; or of what it is to get building work done, even if it be only mud-building work, in a place where there is no poverty compelling enough to persuade people to work at anything for two days running. We had struggled along as best we could while Ponnamal was in Neyoor; but as we had not proper rooms where we could store food-stuffs, we had to buy in small quantities; and there were endless difficulties about getting enough variety for the vegetable diet upon which the health of the children depended. Gradually, as more help came from England, we were able to build nurseries, and so set the old mud rooms free for stores; and Ponnamal, who returned at this point, came into her own.

She added up all the expenses, so multifarious that a Westerner is baffled by them, connected with grain bought straight from the field—buying, carting, husking, cleaning, boiling, drying, storing—and compared these with the cost of rice bought in the bazaar; then she added the cost of the alteration in the store-rooms that would be required if the grain were to be stored by us, and how long it would take to reimburse this expenditure out of our profits; and as she came to the conclusion that, allowing for the numerous items invariably 'forgotten' in an Eastern estimate, we should gain by the change, I handed the whole over to her; and twice a year at the two harvests of the year she saw to the right conduct of all this complicated business, superintended the measuring, and kept the involved accounts. Then there were the smaller and extremely various requirements for curries and condiments, and all the sundries needed for orderly existence. A household as large as ours has to be sufficient to itself, for nothing in any quantity can be bought within a day's journey. All that this fact covers was most capably undertaken by Ponnamal; and I felt sure now that every rupee would do the work of two, or as nearly two as possible.

One morning after her illness had taken fast hold of her, but before she was too ill to be able to think clearly, she went through these items with me, explaining the laws which govern the various markets, and the customs observed in paying the different people employed. The rice measurer, for example, of one field will not measure in another, and each has to be paid in cash and in cloth according to the rules of that particular field. Sugar bought by the sack is to be had at one season; salt, also bought by the sack, at another; rope and cocoanuts and certain oils are cheapest in a town twenty-five miles to the west; curry commodities in another twenty-five miles to the south; and so on—details which, but for her clear-headedness, would have been most bewildering in their minutia, were slowly dictated to me as I took notes of them all. She had an amazing head for figures, and once when she was miserably ill, and I sitting beside her was doing accounts, half aloud, she followed, added up the column of figures, and gave me the correct total. She had helped me to balance my accounts for years, and as long as she could walk came over to my room to do this her last cherished bit of work.

Ponnamal's intimate sharing of all these matters, which to us from the first were sacred secularities, resulted in something of her spirit passing through the whole work. There were some, like Arulai of early days, and others who in these later years have gathered round us, who were naturally nobly-minded, and to them we owe much. But I doubt if we should have that careful thought for economy, which we can truly say exists among us, if it had not been for Ponnamal's example in this matter. No one in Dohnavur looks upon 'the mission' as a limitless fund from which to draw as much as may be of the good things of this life; rather we have difficulty with our girls to get them to take such strength-feeders as milk, for example, when they are under par. More than once after quite a tussle with one who much required it but would not take it, we extracted the protest, 'because the babies need all we ought to buy.' And yet this girl, like every other here, is pouring out all she possesses on the sacrifice and service without a thought of any reward but the joy of doing it.

And as the people around us, to whom our lives are open, watched Ponnamal going about her duty with industry and eagerness, finding in this arduous work all she desired of earthly delight, incorruptible in her integrity, and ever with a lynx eye for waste anywhere, they marvelled at her: 'Such do not exist among us,' they once remarked, summing her up; 'nor did we know there were such among Christians.' They knew that for many unbroken years nothing could draw her away even for a holiday. Some of them knew that she never even told me when any of her relatives were married, because she knew it would trouble me to think of the reproach that would fall upon her if she did not go to the family tamasha; and yet nothing would have persuaded her to go, for there was no one to take her place. It was hidden from us then that soon she would have to go away altogether, and that no one then would take her place. We never thought of ourselves without her. It did not seem possible: she was part of Dohnavur.

CHAPTER 10: AN ORDINARY DAY, AND DIGRESSIONS

Ponnamal's ordinary day began before dawn; for, up till the time of her illness, she saw to the night food of any babies who required it. At that time most of the infants were in one large nursery, under her care; she had of course young girls to help her, but it was she who was responsible; and always she had the sick babies herself. She was a splendid sick-nurse, and knew exactly how to manipulate the food for varyingly constituted babies. 'She knows far more than I do about it,' one of the Neyoor doctors said to me; and as he spoke I recalled a day when she told me how in her extremity she was inwardly directed: 'For the baby "it was Evu who had been at death's door and was still lingering thereabouts" could not take her food, do what I would. She was on Benger, and it had always suited her, but now it failed. I tried weakening it till it contained as little nourishment as I dared to give her; and I tried "digesting" it for a shorter and longer time, but nothing was of any use, and I did not know what to do. And then one day as I stirred in the flour, I lifted my heart once more, and said, "Lord, the inside of this little child is well known to Thee. Guide me, tell me what to do, or she will die!"' And then she told me how, as it seemed to her, the exact number of minutes the food should be 'digested' was suggested to her mind. The directions on the tin were otherwise, but she tried the new way, and immediately Evu began to mend, and recovered perfectly, to become one of our healthiest children.

So, after being up almost invariably several times in the night, Ponnamal's day proper began; and whenever possible it began with short informal prayers with the nurses, at half-past five sometimes in the nursery while the babies slept in the hammocks all round, or in the milk-kitchen, so that the fire-glow fell on the little group kneeling on the floor.

As early as she could get them to come, she was ready for the milk-sellers, and she tested and measured their milk. No one who has not done this sort of thing in the East can imagine all it entails of vigilance. There is not much in India about which there is not a chance to turn a dishonest anna, or, at lowest hope, a pie —a pie being a twelfth of an anna, which is a penny, which is the sixteenth of a rupee. But of all substances, solid or fluid, milk is perhaps the most accommodating, and Ponnamal needed all her nous in dealing with the milk-sellers. 'The mind of the people of this land,' she remarked one day, 'revolves round pies, annas, rupees; rupees, annas, pies.' We knew then that one otherwise minded is rare. We know it with tenfold more emphasis since Ponnamal was taken from us; for we have found it impossible to find anyone able to take her place, even in merely 'secular' ways.

'Have you not one relative or friend you could trust to help you in this work?' we asked the much overburdened Sellamuttu, known elsewhere as Pearl, after a grievous breakdown in good faith on the part of one from outside whom we hoped could have helped. 'Amma,' she answered simply, 'do not expect to find another Ponnamal or even another such as I, by the grace of God, in the matter of truth now am; for such you will not find.'

After the milk-buying came the food-making. For years Ponnamal did this entirely herself. And till we had our own English nurse she was always the one to help me in making up the medicines if any were needed. Her clear head was of wonderful assistance in working out the doses in correct proportions. But here again, as in the housekeeping matter, I feel hardly one in a thousand will realize what it meant to have her help.

Take a concrete case, one of scores: Preena, the Elf, was ill with enteric. The Walkers had just gone home, and the night they left, the only sound in the house was the moaning of the delirious child. I remember how empty the house felt, and how silent, and yet it was not empty or silent. Those who had to leave us were not forgetting us as their bullock-carts trundled off; and we were not alone. But the nursing of typhoid night and day, even with a doctor to pilot one through, must always be arduous work; without a doctor, it is, to put it briefly, killing. Toward the end of the time,

48

the child, who had been doing well, suddenly developed a new trouble. Her throat seemed to shut up, and for three days she swallowed nothing. I searched desperately through Moore's *Manual of Family Medicine* and Birch's *Management of Children in India*, our two standbys here, but found nothing relevant to her condition; and with eyes that could hardly see the print pored over the four columns of *A Dictionary of Domestic Medicine and Surgery*, by Dr. Thompson and Dr. Steele, which ponderous volume sometimes showed us the way we should go. All in vain; Preena had walked out of the pages devoted to her malady in all three books. It is a dreadful way children in India have, this branching off into vagaries in illness. 'What does the book say about it?' 'It says nothing at all!' How often we go through that experience of despair. Months later, in an old edition of Moore, I found a small-print note to the effect that a certain swelling of the glands of the neck is a possible, though unusual, complication in enteric. But that day I found nothing.

Think of what it was at such a time to have one like Ponnamal alongside, able to look after all I had to leave undone, and ready, too, to make up the medicines for the village people; for we had what was almost a village dispensary in those days. It was rest to the tired-out mind to feel she could not if she tried make a mistake in a calculation, so accurately did her clear brain work; all would be correct to the fraction of a minim.

This gift of precision was one for which my soul sang many a Benedicite. Who that has had to diagnose an infant, hunt through medical books for corresponding symptoms, make up the very minute doses, and give them, and all in what sometimes was tearing anxiety, but will appreciate the comfort of such help? In the earlier days of the work, as I have said, some very miscellaneous children were sent to us—weakly, diseased, hurt little mortals. We could not refuse them, though they were not the kind of child we existed to save; we had to do our best for them all. Some died, but others throve; and on the whole, doctorless as we still are, we are a very healthy family.

Ponnamal was rather wonderful, too, in the way she learned to appreciate methods which to her were entirely new and crudely Western. The Indian mind is made of folds, firmly folded in unexpected places. You despair of ever winning to the far end of it, there are so many plies in it, as Samuel Rutherford said in a different connection, and Ponnamal's mind was Indian. The first time I remember our differing about anything vital was when I wanted the babies to sleep in the open air. Ponnamal had been brought up in the usual Indian fashion; a stuffy little room with every window carefully shut at night was her idea of things as they should be. As soon as possible we built airy rooms, with verandahs on which the children could sleep; and life was made as much out of door as possible; and Ponnamal, in her loving solicitude for the babies, feared this very much, and the creases within were evident. But I knew she would speedily iron them all out, and waited in peace. Presently I saw her do it; and she soon became as keen about fresh air for the children as we were. When her own little daughter came from school with signs of tubercle upon her, she threw herself heartily into the fresh-air treatment, and Purripu grew into a healthy girl. 'Look at Purripu,' her mother would say to anyone who, dismayed by our new-fangled ways, cheerfully prophesied chronic colds ending in premature death all round. 'She was thin and stooping six months ago, and always tired. Now look at her!'

But this is a digression, though belonging in spirit to the ordinary day.

As long as she could, Ponnamal had a Bible-class with her young nurses in the forenoons; but as the work grew, this became impossible. And it hardly mattered; for her whole life was a lesson. No girl, however naturally self-centred or indolent, could be with her without catching something of her brave unselfish spirit; a spirit that toiled unto weariness every day it lived, and cared for nothing but the children's good.

In the afternoon, if all were well, she went to her own little room behind the nursery, and rested for an hour. But if a baby were ill, or any other anxiety pressed, it was hard to get her to rest; if her heart were anxious, her body could not rest. Then came the evening milk to be tested and measured, and the night foods to be made, and so the ordinary day ended.

But how little of it I have told! There were so many other things tucked into its corners—little acts of helpfulness, careful thoughts that worked out into some new economy or some new endeavour—that a book might be written about them alone. For example, while she was measuring the milk, a servant would pass, and she would call him aside for a moment and say a word or two. And the next thing we who had to see to the larger matters of life were aware of, was some pieces of work about which we had consulted together, accomplished, or set on foot. She had that faculty, as rare as *nous*, the power to get things done. And in a land where a workman comes, bargains about the work, says he will do it to-morrow, takes the inevitable advance without which a carpenter cannot mend a stool, or a potter make a pot, or a mason build a house, and then goes away, finds a distant relative has just deceased, goes to the funeral, and forgets to come back till you have spent what ought to have been his wages on coolies to go and search for him, this faculty is invaluable.

Then there were those other days, when everything seemed to go wrong on purpose: 'Piria Sittie is learning how upsetting things can be in India,' Ponnamal said once about Miss Wade, who was experiencing what the land can do in the way of heaping up difficulties. Or if, later, the newly launched little school were plunging about in troubled waters, she would sympathize, and lend a helping hand by trying to replan the nursery work so as to make the dove-tailing of the two halves of the family a little easier to compass. Or we would be suddenly involved in some tangle of circumstances, where her sagacity was required to find the way out; or perhaps it was a battle for a child—a battle in the heavenlies, to be fought out on our knees; or something needing for its handling the very wisdom of God. Whichever it was, Ponnamal, as I have said before, was ready. Many a wise and silent raid upon the kingdom of darkness was thought out by her, and often she led it herself. Once she came back in triumph with a baby in her arms, about whom the town—a famous Temple town—was so stirred that it all but rose in streets, but did not; for the quieting hand of our God was upon it.

But that last was a strange experience. The child's mother, knowing the peril to which her little babe was exposed, put it herself in Ponnamal's arms with the hurried whisper, 'Hasten out before you are waylaid.' Ponnamal knew well that if she were, the angry hunters after such prey would coerce the mother into denying what she had done. She knew the upshot would be a false case, with all the paraphernalia of witnesses ranged ready to forswear themselves for four annas a head. And she knew how such things end; what she had done would be a crime—she knew right well its penalty. But not even the word *prison*, a word that strikes the Tamil heart cold, held terrors for her. In a work like this, open at all times to attack which no ingenuity of man or woman could avoid or repel, was it not something to have for a fellow-worker one to whom the word 'fear' was a word unknown?

Only once I saw her shrink. It was when the shadow that is never far from us seemed about to close round me. She did not seem able to bear it. A thousand times Yes to it, if she were the one to be engulfed—for the one she loved it was different. But she came to be willing for even that, if thereby a child could be saved; and beyond that I know of no more loyal, perfect love.

CHAPTER 11: AHEAD OF HER GENERATION

The years of search, and of service, and of shouldering what to her had been large responsibilities, developed all that was fine in Ponnamal. She had always been remarkable for earnestness, but now there was a new air of sure-footedness about her. She had learnt to walk in slippery places without slipping. Her judgment had ripened, too; I found myself turning more and more confidently to her for counsel in difficult hours.

So also, apparently, did the people about us; for they brought all manner of matters to her, from the maladies of their babies to the marriages of their daughters. I used to wonder sometimes how they regarded her views on the latter subject; Ponnamal could be caustic when she chose.

It was she who explained to me the mysteries of the marriage market. In India we do not buy our brides as do the barbarous: we buy our bridegrooms; and in our part of the country the price, called by courtesy daughter's dowry, is arranged on a sliding scale according to the examinations passed by the suitor, so much per examination or 'failed pass.' Thus a B.A. is so much, a 'failed B.A.' so much, next come a 'First Arts' and a 'failed F.A.' then 'Matriculate' and 'failed Matric.' The plan is simple, but it spells ruin for a parent who wants to marry his girls to educated men, and Ponnamal considered it wrong every way. But she was far ahead of her generation on the whole subject; she disapproved, for example, of girls being committed to the irrevocable fact of marriage before they knew their own minds, and she thought the marriage question should be lifted up into a higher atmosphere, and approached in a finer spirit than that common now. She had other thoughts too, even rarer; for she held that India needed the service of the unmarried woman as well as of the married; and that the time must come when this would be acknowledged by the Church in India. She never compared the relative holiness or devotion required for the two kinds of service; she simply held that India needed both, and that there was work to do which only one who was free to be 'absorbed in her duties towards her Lord' "I quote from Mr. Arthur Way's translation of 1 Cor. vii. 34" could do; and indeed the proof of this lay all about us.

'When it is taught that the Cross is the attraction,' she said, quoting a favourite word of ours "whose truth she did not think was much taught now", 'things will be altogether different.' She knew that for many sacrifice would be found in the bringing up of a family for the highest ends; but for some she believed it would surely lead to a turning from the greatest human joy for the sake of those who must otherwise be left to perish. All this, even this last, which as yet in our community is not recognized as true or possible or even desirable, Ponnamal said when occasion arose, in her usual incisive fashion; and courage and her principles were tested. While Purripu was still young, hardly more than a school-girl, a suitor was suggested by some members of her family. The dowry difficulty could be overcome, as there was money obtainable if only Ponnamal would compromise a little, in the matter of putting jewels on her daughter, and in other small concessions to the spirit of the world. But that was not Ponnamal's way.

Later, when her illness made the matter of Purripu's future one of serious concern, she was assailed on all sides; relatives, friends, neighbours, even the most unlikely came to see her about it, and they wearied her spirit exceedingly. For by this time the mother knew her daughter's mind, and to Purripu the desire had come to follow in her mother's steps and take up what she could of the work that must soon be laid down. Should she be forced to abandon it? Ponnamal faced it out. She only wanted to obey; she knew that 'obedience leads to unexpected places and knows no precedents;' there was no precedent for her guidance now, and the mother-love in her could not rest without some clear sign from her Lord. Alone in hospital she was given such a sign. It was of the kind that could not be controverted. And to the credit of her relatives be it told, that when once they knew of it they left her in peace, and all her prayer for Purripu from that day forward was that she might go on in strength. 'Let not her crown be tarnished, Lord,' was the sum of all she asked.

But it was not her mind on these subjects which interested our neighbours, who liked her better when she met them on their own ground, which after all is the most we can usually do for the rank and file of our own generation. You cannot pull people uphill who do not want to go: you can only point up. So she listened patiently to their long involved and explicit descriptions of symptoms, cause, never mere result, of discrepancies within; and to the much-tried mothers of many infants she was an angel from heaven.

It was in the morning and evening chiefly, when the milk-sellers came, that Ponnamal held her clinics. Up would come an agitated mother, with a brass vessel of milk in one hand and a baby in the other. The milk tested, measured, and poured out, the baby would be introduced. Then if business allowed it, Ponnamal would go into its matters and, amid yards of talk from the mother, interrupted by many remarks from the baby, extract as many facts as she could. Or, it would be a stolid four-year-old, clothed in a bead and a bangle, who, too disgusted for speech, would be solemnly spread on its parent's knee, and poked in divers places till a squeal announced the discovery of some vulnerable point.

Among Ponnamal's books is one of dilapidated appearance, a translation into Tamil of a simple medical book written in 1860 by one Edward Waring, Physician to the Maharajah of Travancore. In it, clearly set forth, are many maladies with their appropriate treatment, so far as a lay person can attempt to treat them. Where that is undesirable the fact is noted; but where bazaar remedies can help, such are suggested, and the stumbler in these obscure regions is guided in the way he should go. This book, with, as commentary thereupon, Ponnamal's experience at Neyoor, furnished her, ingenious and common-sensed person that she was, with the means to help many, and her fame as a medico was great. One day she received the following English letter, written in one long paragraph:

'DEAR SISTER,

'Though we had no personal talk yet I think you could recollect me. I hear you are doing the service of God: very good. I am doing medical practice privately too. I treat cases. I have got very efficacious medicines for diabetes, leprosy, asthma, etc., and diseases considered to be hopeless. Some medicines were taught and given by a Yogi [Hindu ascetic]. He is a graduate, and was drawing four hundred rupees a month from Government and had children also. He made arrangements for their maintenance and left everything; he is in Benares practising religious life. Nothing happens in the world without the will of God. I am a daily communicant and was inspired to write you these few lines. In addition to your work do you like to do "qualified" medical practice? It will be very useful. If you like I can get you a diploma from Colombo for the medical practice. You can learn it yourself if I send you the books. The cost of the books is five rupees. The medicines are made into globules and given electricity power. For every disease there are numbers; 1, 2, 3, etc., and according to the number you must prescribe the medicine for each disease. You can learn it in no time. To diagnose disease you must go through our materia medica. This business will not tire you much, and you can get many friends if you begin to practise. I am the commission agent for this district. I have got medicine chests containing all the medicines for all the diseases for ten rupees. If you require an order I can send to you.

If you require any other informations I am ready to give you.'

The letter concluded with moral reflections: 'Where there is a will there is a way.' 'Our life is like a cloud rapidly vanishing,' and so on. The humours of life in the East are unfailing.

CHAPTER 12: SACRED SECULARITIES

From the first day of our work together, I had shared everything concerning the children with Ponnamal; she was fellow-worker, not under-worker, a difference which causes things to be which otherwise could never be. Memories of experiences thus mutual crowd upon me, and that practical thing, money, is mixed up in some of the first and in some of the last.

When Ponnamal joined us, she had property the produce of which was sufficient to make her independent. This was quietly appropriated by her guardian, and to get it she would have had to go to law. But to go to law before the unbelievers, with as defendant a relative in mission employ, seemed to her impossible; so she suffered herself to be defrauded. This, which was distinctly for Christ's sake, wrought in her that quality which results in a pure spirit towards money: it had no power over her; and when the Temple children's work began, this in her was most precious to me.

Before this special work began we had no financial responsibilities. If the money for itinerating work had stopped, it would only have meant that some of the villages we had hoped to visit would have been dropped. But children cannot be dropped in that calm fashion; and quite early we learned the wholesome lesson not to look to man or woman, but to God, the living God, for the continuation as well as for the beginning of everything; and we never thought of any gift as something which might be repeated. Still, though we never had, and never have had, any 'supported children,' whatever is sent being used for the next need, some refused to understand this, and kindly insisted in considering themselves responsible for individual children. One day, from such a one came a letter saying that she was sorry she 'found it impossible to send anything for her child this year; there were so many claims.' Ponnamal's smile over that letter was untroubled: 'But does she think the baby will stop living for a year?' she asked rather mischievously. Or, again, spasmodic charities enlivened our accounts: broke our rule, and counted on it; I can feel even now the cheerful feeling of that minute. The paroxysm of sympathy passed. Something was sent, a large and welcome gift; and then pet dogs proved more absorbing an interest than babies in peril. But from the first we had seen our way clear before us with regard to this matter. No one on earth had authorized the work; no one, then, could in fairness be counted responsible. But if, as we believed, our Father in Heaven had laid His commands upon us, to Him we had a right to look for all that was needed for the carrying out of those commands; so that our only care was to be attentive to His wishes.

This looks an easy condition, and in one way it was easy, but in another difficult. Who that has known the discipline of perplexity will speak of such discipline as easy?

But next to the quickening experiences of great joy and great grief I know of nothing which leads more directly to the heart of our Father than just this sense of perplexity. 'I am but a little child: I know not how to go out or come in.' And the speech pleased the Lord, and He made it His pleasure to help His servant. We at least found it so.

And constantly as we went on we had proof of that which I can only call an intimate loving-kindness, a care to which nothing is minute. The very passing of the thought of one's heart was noted. 'Before the birth of the word in my tongue,' as our Tamil idiom has it, 'Thou hast known it all.' Such knowledge is too wonderful for me. It is like nothing so much as the knowledge which comes from the study under the microscope of what in Dohnavur we call a 'rich' drop of water. It is high in its lowliness, we cannot attain unto it. And truly when one considers that there is provision whereby a water creature from whom the water is receding "and all he wants is the fraction of a drop to make him happy" can roll himself into a ball, and preserve his vitality, though in a state of utter dustiness for years, it becomes nothing short of blasphemous to be faithless about the affairs of little immortals, with histories too, like those of these children for whom the Lord their Redeemer has already fought such battles. It is easier, looked at fairly, to have faith than to fear. So at least it seemed to us one day towards the end of Ponnamal's illness, when a letter of good cheer came which comforted us both; and as she lay with that letter in her hands, its very paper a pleasant thing to touch and caress, she told me then that the night before, when she was awake with pain, and everything looked as black as night, she had thought about the difficulties ahead when the children would grow up. In other parts of India there could not be the same difficulties "with, concealed inside them, pitfalls": she had travelled and she knew. We seemed to have been set in, humanly speaking, the most impossible place for an endeavour of this sort. And she felt that the need for faith about temporal things was as nothing to the need of it where these spiritual things are concerned; 'For it was as if I saw you called to bear heavier anxieties than we have ever borne together' "unknown to her a bitterer cup than we had ever before tasted was even then being prepared for us". 'But as I thought of this, distressed, I saw you as the tamarind tree out there, blown about by many storms and with nothing on earth to lean upon, but only rooting the deeper; and I was comforted for you, for I saw the Lord with you in the future, and I knew each little child would be precious in His sight.'

Some months after that talk, and after Ponnamal had been long enough in Paradise to have learned by a thousand blessed proofs that nothing she could expect of her Lord could be too kind for Him to do, a letter came to the house, upon another matter, but concluding with words so brave, so comforting in their calm assurance, that I found myself unawares reading them aloud to Ponnamal. The letter was from a C.M.S. secretary, till then a friend unknown: 'Your ministry has in it such possibilities of blessing for the souls and bodies of those little ones for whom Christ died, that we dare not have a moment's anxiety or doubt as to its fruitfulness and far-reaching influence.' '*That we dare not*': Praise God for faith like this.

I do not know if it was given to our dear Ponnamal to hear the words I read; if they could make her happier, I am sure they were made known to her; but I have written them in this her story because they seem to me to belong to it.

CHAPTER 13: OUR ARM EVERY MORNING

We have come now to the year 1912. There are some dates that do not fly. The time down to the minute lives with me.

It was Saturday, August 21, at half-past eight in the morning. A civilian, keen on music, had been staying with us, and instead of departing at seven as he had intended, he had gone to the big schoolroom with us, and we with the children had been singing English hymns. The bright little picture stands out clear—Miss Wade at the organ; the children, to whom every white man is a mixture of hero, saint, and playfellow, pressing round; flowers looking in at the window and down from the roof, for a climbing allamanda, with its large soft yellow flowers, grew in between the top of the wall and the roof, and hung its bells overhead. We finished with 'The King of Love,' and then came joyfully up to the house, the children as usual all excitement to see the motor-cycle start. On the dining-room table lay the letters—and a telegram: 'Walker dangerously ill.'

Mr. Walker had gone to the Telugu country to take meetings. Mrs. Walker was in England. This telegram which had been delayed for two days was the first intimation we had had of any trouble. Five hours later, the second telegram came: 'And they shall see His face; and His Name shall be in their foreheads.'

Can words tell what Ponnamal was to us all through that time? For some days the compound was besieged by crowds of people, who, appeared at intervals and roamed about noisily, raising clouds of dust, and filling the place with unquietness. Ponnamal helped us to soothe and disperse them. Then, when at last we were left to our grief, grief for the one in England, the children, ourselves—for in this order it advanced upon us—to me, stripped as I verily felt I was at that moment of my strongest earthly stay, she said: 'It must be that you are meant to lean on God alone.'

At first it seemed as if we might hold on, but could not dare to develop further: it felt impossible to face the anxiety of growing bigger. This will not be understood by the brave and self-reliant souls of whom fortunately the world contains so many; nor will it be clearly intelligible to any except those few who know the conditions under which we work. This attack on the hidden heart of a system dominant in India for centuries carries in itself possibilities unknown to the nearest friend outside it. It is quite different from any other work known to me in twenty-four years of life abroad; quite different too, of course, from any sort of philanthropic work, in much of which Hindus themselves are genuinely interested. On the surface what we are doing looks usual enough; and to visitors who see nothing of the shapes behind the children, it is all quite obvious and pretty. But those shapes are always visible to us, and to Ponnamal they were visible always. It was with relation to this, the undefinable, the inexplicable, that Mr. Walker's presence had been such a strength and help to us.

He knew India as few know it; he was wise as few are wise; and he had that rarest gift of never failing one at a crisis. And then, too, his sympathies were bound up in the work; the children were not just 'the children' to him—they might have been his own; he thought of them so tenderly, and so individually, that one could always go to him and talk over matters connected with their varying characters, sure of his interest, the interest of one to whom the matter in hand really belongs. 'I have no man like-minded who will naturally care for your state:' how often the word has come to me since that good friend departed.

Ponnamal realized this from the first. It was in her mind when she said, 'It must be that you are meant to lean on God alone.' And then gradually I understood that what had been rather a trouble to me at times was now to be a comfort. For often, when in times of uncertainty I went to the little study for advice, I had to come away without it. 'I don't know anything about it,' he would say; for he was not one of those who never say, 'I don't know.' It was as if often he could only help by turning to his Lord, and asking Him to help us; and was not that one way left open to him still? More and more as I pondered it the curious fact emerged that, though I had hardly realized it, so perfect had his sympathy been, yet he had never once taken the initiative or the responsibility in any matter concerning the work; he had not ever advised where its more intricate problems were concerned, for they touched upon things in that Underland life which he knew was beyond his ken. He had championed us; and to that championship we owed much of our freedom from molestation. He had sympathized with us in a way which halved every grief and doubled every joy. But that which was essential to the continuance of the work did not depend on him, but on the One who dieth no more. A friend sent me just then a Mildmay text, 'Thou remainest;' and a Dohnavur comrade painted in blue letters on brown teak, 'Be Thou their arm every morning;' these words were comfort and strength to me.

And to my dear Ponnamal too. For in all this she shared, as indeed did every one of our united household. Of them all, Ponnamal was the only one whose knowledge of the conditions of this land fitted her to be counsellor. But she had been left, and our treasure, Arulai, was with us too; and I was ashamed of the feeling of bereftness that had at first laid hold on me in spite of the multitude of comforts that had refreshed my soul. So we went on. And to our astonishment—so foolish are we and ignorant—that which we had thought we could not do, we did, God being our Arm every morning.

CHAPTER 14: HER PAIN

It was Friday, March 28, of the following year, another of those dates that can never be forgotten. Ponnamal had been ailing for some weeks, but no premonition of serious trouble disturbed us; our chief anxiety was a sick baby. In the intervals of life I was trying to get 'Walker of Tinnevelly' written, and one day, that day, into the middle of it plunged an excited messenger: 'Ponnamal has a bad pain, it has seized her suddenly! Can you come?' Before the end of the description of that pain was in sight, I was with Ponnamal.

There is so much suffering and sorrow in the world just now that I think hearts must be too sore to bear needless medical detail, so two years and five months shall go into a paragraph.

It was cancer; an operation stayed matters for a while. There were, however, complications which detained us in hospital for three months. We returned home thankful and hopeful. But Ponnamal soon began to suffer more. Treatment, operative and other, failed to do more than give temporary ease. So matters continued till October 5, 1914, when we were told cancer had returned and that nothing could be done. In one way it was a relief to know that the misery of more operations was to be spared her. But she suffered, with only occasional respite, till August 26, 1915, when she was released from the body of this death.

And now memories crowd upon me: which shall I take and show?

A room with a bed in it, and beside the bed a table with a shaded lantern on it. Ponnamal lies on the bed breathing so quietly that in the dim light I can hardly see if the sheet moves with her breath. It is the first night after her operation, and she is half unconscious yet. Suddenly into the stillness of the night, startling one with the weirdness of it, pours forth a torrent of prayer—prayer for the doctors who had tried to help her; for me—and the utter love in the words brings the tears stinging into my eyes for the children, her little beloveds; name after name pours out, as child after child comes up in her faithful memory. At last she stops, exhausted; her pulse seems to me in my terrible anxiety to fail. Should I call the doctor, who had told me to call him if there were any change? But he is tired after a long day's work, and I think longingly of our one trained nurse at home on furlough who would give all she possessed to be here now; and so the hours pass till the welcome morning dawns, and with it hope.

Weeks have passed since that night. Ponnamal is facing another operation, calm and quiet; but within is a very disappointed heart. The post has brought a letter from Dohnavur, and we are reading it together. It is from Arulai, fragile in body, and even then on the edge of illness, but triumphant in spirit. She is in charge at Dohnavur, helped by all who are there, but still the one upon whom the heaviest burden falls. She has been counting, not in days, but in hours and in minutes to the time of our return. This new trouble has moved it, who can tell how far off? This is what she writes: 'Are you tasting the sweetness of this time? I am.' And light comes back to Ponnamal. She too 'tastes the sweetness of the time.'

And now bright, golden memory; a bullock-cart, moving slowly round the mountains' foot; and in the cart Ponnamal, looking out with rejoicing eyes. 'I never expected to see them again,' she says, as she watches the hills soften and darken against a yellow sky; and she tells me how on that last day at Dohnavur she had balanced her accounts so as to leave all straight for me. And as she talks, my heart shakes with mighty throbs of thankfulness that I have her warm and living beside me.

I see a compound now in the early joyful morning, freshened by the first June rains, its greens and terra-cottas mingling happily, its calm encircling hills half asleep in sleepy mists. Then there is a shout and a rush; everywhere little blue figures are dancing about us, and the air is full of laughter; and Ponnamal is, lifted out of the cart and carried in; and there are palms up everywhere, and flowers.

And again, a great waste field; but even as I look at it, it grows into an ordered garden with rows of plantains—banana is the word that gives the sense of the undulating green which is its glory. And up and down among the plants Ponnamal is walking, still unsteadily, but rejoicing to be walking at all. A tent is pitched near the well where a pair of bullocks draw water for the field; the splash of the falling water fills the picture with a sense of coolness. Soon Ponnamal, wearied but happy, walks slowly to the tent and rests.

It was a constant joy to us so to see her in this garden of her own creation, blessed help through the days when her heart would not let her be without doing something for the general good, but her head could not bear the noise and movement of the nursery. Ponnamal's garden, it will always be called; it is in fruit now, and we wonder if she sees, and is pleased.

And for last—late Christmas Eve: the nursery with its whitewashed walls and red-tiled floor; a lamp is burning low; a sick child gazing far away with that aloof look in her eyes that says, 'I belong to another country.' And watching her, with arms that ache to take her and nurse her back to life, Ponnamal. For she has crawled up to the nursery, constrained thither by the love in her; and now exhausted by the effort, but serene in the victory of her spirit over the oppressive and reluctant flesh, she sits stifling the groan that breaks from her—type, though she little dreams it, of that which lights the ages as star-shine a black night: the imperishable quality of Love.

CHAPTER 15: HER MUSIC

It was in that same Christmas week that Ponnamal heard for the first time what she always described as her music. She was at that time taking aspirin, a drug which up till a little later was sufficient to keep the worst pain under. She took it every six hours, and when the time drew near for taking it could hardly wait for it, though she disciplined herself to wait with a will that never faltered. But when her music began she entirely forgot it. She described the music variously: sometimes she seemed to recognize voices singing familiar words; then at other times it was only music, but such melodious sound that she wanted to lie awake all night and listen to it. This she could never do. Within ten minutes of its beginning she was asleep, and she would sleep the whole night through, and wake refreshed, not having touched medicine. There was never any need for her to tell us when she had heard this music: her face told us; the old beaming smile would return, and we would hear again the merry care-free laugh. It was as if she had bathed in the night in the waters of immortality, and been renewed.

The good thing wrought in her was so apparent that a guest of the time doubted the correctness of the sentence of death that had been passed upon her. There was no outward sign of illness; was it credible that anyone in the grip of such a disease could be like this? A few minutes' 'music,' a single night's reprieve from pain, could hardly account for such exaltation of spirit, and above all such a sense of health; and it seemed as if Ponnamal began to think so too.

One morning, after a night of restful sleep, she felt so well that we walked round the compound together, and she noticed as usual things that should be put right. A heavy branch in the great tamarind tree was not safe, and she suggested a way by which it might be propped up. While we were considering it, the church-bell began to toll, and she remarked calmly, 'The village people will think it is for me.' The word caught at something in me, and she knew it. 'Don't be troubled,' she said, and stopped to pour loving, reassuring words upon me; 'perhaps we shall go together; not now, but when the work for the children is finished.' But severe suffering followed upon this; and her hope faded.

Once, after a long silent interval, she heard her music in the afternoon, which was unusual. She fell asleep as she listened to it, and woke after two hours, feeling, as she said, quite well. And she got up at once and dressed eagerly, hardly daring to believe in her reprieve. Then, as it still continued, she walked to the upper part of the compound, where some new nurseries were being built. There, charmed afresh by the beauty of it, she stood gazing across to the mountains and then round about her at the flowers. For our compound enclosed in its walls is like a great garden; all manner of lovely things grow happily in it, its trees are always green. People coming into it from the dried-up land beyond have wondered at its greenness; and so, indeed, did we, till, a few days ago, some workmen sinking an artesian well struck a river flowing fifty feet below the surface. Back in the far ages that river had been caused to flow from the western mountains, through the heart of the wide field, that was set apart for us; and now its streams make glad our little city of God.

'It is like a new world to me,' said Ponnamal, as she walked slowly round the big circle reserved for a playground, and looked at the nurseries grouped about it; and behind them to the mountains, lighted now in sunset colours. She had spent many days in her room, and though it was kept like a little bower, this was different; she did not know how to enjoy it enough. And the thought that must have passed through a thousand minds shaped afresh in ours: If earth can be so beautiful, what must the heavenly places be?

The next night she heard her music again. She told the girls who were with her at the time, and who heard nothing, to be quiet that she might listen; and as usual she left her medicine untouched. She woke next morning saying, 'Why do the cocks crow so soon?' a remark which amused her immensely when she was awake enough to understand what she had said; for the most welcome of all sounds to her through those months was the crowing of the cocks that told the long night was nearly over.

I have thought sometimes that, if we had only our recollection to depend upon, we might doubt now, lest our imagination were painting the grey facts of that painful time—and to colour facts is criminal. But this note, one of several, is sufficiently definite; it is dated January 21, 1915. 'Ponnamal had a wonderful night. Music and singing, then sleep, from 9 p.m. till 5 a.m. She woke so happy that involuntarily she clapped her hands for joy. She thinks that Lulla "a five-year-old child who left us for Paradise, clapping her hands with unmistakable delight" must have had some such experience of happiness when she clapped her hands.'

Another entry of about the same date records how she had herself wondered if it could be imagination; but after it had been frequently repeated, and each time so effectually banished her pain that she had no need of medicine, she came to believe it was something real, and after listening to the words of a hymn "'How sweet the Name of Jesus sounds'", sung, as she thought, by ten or fifteen voices, she gave up all question, and took it to be the kindness of her Lord that allowed her to overhear a little of the music of the Land of Song, to whose borders she had come.

For ourselves, we accepted it as among the many things of life which we may only know in part until for us too the curtain of sense wears thin; and we had long since learned to set no limits to the dealings of the Lord with His beloved. But we began to wonder if things as yet hidden from us were contained in this illness; and when one came to the house who was earnest about following the primitive Church custom of anointing the sick, Ponnamal being desirous, she was anointed. We could not be sure that the answer to our prayers would be health restored. We should have felt it unchildlike, unbecoming, to be peremptory with our most loving Father, or even perpetually insistent. Not 'Thy will be changed,' but 'Thy will, be done,' was the prayer given to us to pray. And we laid a palm branch across her bed as she lay waiting, in token that either way it would be victory.

From that day forward, Ponnamal grew rapidly worse, and we knew that we were answered: 'What I do thou knowest not now; but thou shalt know hereafter.'

CHAPTER 16: IN THE MIDST OF THE FURNACE

And it was victory, though that victory was not always apparent at the time. And because to-day there are many called to stand on the outer side of just such fires, I will try to set down that which every now and then was shown to us for our comfort, till we learned that for those who suffer in righteousness there is appointed an angel of the Lord who smites the flame of the fire out of the furnace, and makes in the midst of the furnace as it had been a moist whistling wind, so that the fire cannot touch them at all, neither hurt nor trouble them—though indeed for the moment, to us who observe them, things may seem far otherwise.

We had not, at the time I am thinking, of now, used morphia; aspirin still sufficed to keep things tolerable. But that drug ran short, and a substitute was supplied which was useless. I wired to those of our family who were on the hills—for it was our hot season and they had to be away—and they sent a supply of the right medicine to us as soon as possible; but the five days which passed before it came were such that at last we had to give a hypodermic, only to find that the morphia recently supplied had lost its power. Those who have lived through such a time will know how every minute sensation bites into the soul, etched into it as with a red-hot needle.

But now for the comfort: Ponnamal told me afterwards that when the pain was at its height it was as if the Lord Himself stood by her, quoting to her familiar words; and she said, 'The waters did not overflow me, nor did the flame kindle on me; no, never once.' There had been no indication that things were so. All we had seen was a poor, tormented, or at best stupefied body, a house with its blinds drawn down, whose words, when there was speech at all, were only about its pain.

Later, when we were together again, she longed for her music; and one evening one of her Sitties played softly at some little distance from her room, hoping by suggestion, if it might be so, to woo those sweet strains back to her. Did the angels smile tenderly on our poor attempts, I wonder? Ponnamal did. 'I heard the baby organ last night,' she remarked next morning. 'Did it ease you? Did it make you sleep?' and she turned her great, dark, loving eyes upon us and smiled. And then, fearing she had been ungrateful, she said, 'It was Prémie Sittie, was it not? Indeed, I enjoyed listening.' But she never spoke of it as resembling that other music, which never came now.

Sometimes she was a little troubled because she had none of the ecstatic feelings she had read that others had when death was near; and one day, when we were talking about walking by faith, and of the mark of His confidence it was when our God trusted us to do it and to be content to do it, she said: 'Yes, I know that is what I am to do; for the life to come is as a sealed book to me. I do not fear, I have peace, but I have no feeling of great joy: all is silent and sealed.' This continued to be so till one night a comforting dream was granted. Early in the morning long before dawn she sent for me; she could not wait till morning to tell it. She was sinking, she said, in a deep stream, and the weeds grew thick and entangled her, and she called, and instantly the Lord Himself was with her, and the next moment—but 'a moment' does not express the instantaneousness of it—she was with Him. Then she began to praise, saying, 'Amen. Blessing, and glory, and wisdom, and thanksgiving, and honour, and power, and might, be unto our God for ever and ever. Amen.' And then thinking I was there, she turned to me. 'O my mother, where are the children?' she asked; and awoke on earth again. But the seals of the book had been broken by the gladness of that bright dream.

As often as we could through those months she had what Samuel Rutherford calls the comfort of 'Christ's fair moonlight in His word and Sacraments.' Hallowed hours those were, set in stillness, and filled with a peace that neither pain nor grief nor any fear could touch. When, in the days that came after, the waters compassed her about, even unto the soul, and the depths closed her round about, and the weeds were wrapped about her head, she would recall her light, and in the strength of her Risen Lord forbid the darkness to engulf her. Thus, receiving abundance of grace, she reigned in life by One Christ Jesus.

She was still as clear in brain as ever. The storms of pain that swept over her, the large doses of depressing drugs she had to take, appeared to have no ill-effect on her wonderfully powerful mind. She followed the war news closely, and to her the story of the angels at Mons which reached us long before the news-papers had begun to argue over it, was natural, not wonderful; and so was the still more intimate account of the White Comrade. But when the gallant young brother of one of the Sitties was left wounded on the field, and 'Missing' was the only word that came to us about him, then the thought of the War became too personal and poignant, and we had to keep its heavy shadow from her: she had not strength to bear it. Almost to the end she heard all the family news; advised with her old wisdom; was still in all ways her loving, ardent, eager self. So full of vitality she was that it seemed as if she could not die.

Once while I was reading to her from the Song of Songs, a book which was as honey in the comb to her, she laughed with joy. We had just read the verse, 'Who is she that cometh up from the wilderness leaning upon her Beloved?' when she exclaimed, 'Oh, that is a happy word!' and she told me that a few nights before, when the medicine failed to give her sleep, she lay tossing about and turning from side to side, finding ease nowhere, till at last she cried aloud and said, 'O my compassionate Lord, I want to rejoice, but I cannot. The air is hot, and my bed is hot, and the pain is weariness to me.' And it was as if He came quickly very near her and soothed her, telling her He understood; and reminding her of this very word, He told her she was coming up out of the wilderness, not long to stay in it. 'Because the way is short, I thank Thee, Lord'—and yet she was not hurried in spirit to go; she was far more eager to stay, if only she could help us by staying. But the human part of her stood on tip-toe to be off, and once she said longingly, speaking of Christiana and how she received her token, an arrow with a point sharpened with love let easily into her heart, 'It is a long ten days since I received my token, and I am not away yet. When will the good day come?'

One morning Purripu, who was one of her devoted nurses, brought her a great vase of unopened violet passion-flowers, trained in light sprays over branches of henna, our Indian mignonette. 'Watch; they will open at nine o'clock,' she said, as she put the vase on the table beside her mother. And Ponnamal watched; and just before nine o'clock the interlaced filaments began to stir as if conscious of the time, and by the hour appointed all the flowers were open. Ponnamal had long known the ways of Passion-flowers, but the morning hours are busy in the nursery, and she had never had leisure to watch the little moving miracle. 'Just at the hour we keep holy as the hour He was crucified, His flower of Sorrow opens, and shows all mysteries,' she said; and her thoughts travelled back to Calvary, and she sucked sweet comfort from the word that tells us we have not a High Priest who cannot be touched with the feeling of our infirmities. Her room was full of the scent of the flowers when a little later I was with her, and in her face was peace.

'Words I have known all my life have a new force within them now,' she said suddenly one day; and she told how a great dread had been upon her, lest when, near the end, the pain grew more violent, and her will weaker to endure, she would not be able to bear it. And once when this fear oppressed her, almost like a voice speaking aloud, the words of the promise reassured her: 'God is faithful, who will not suffer you to be tempted above that ye are able; but will with the temptation also make a way of escape, that ye may be able to bear it.' That negative verb, which in Tamil idiom has it that God will not give room for such a thing to happen, was an immense comfort to Ponnamal, and she took delight in Ridley's words to Latimer: 'Be of good cheer, brother; for God will either assuage the fury of the flame, or strengthen us to abide it.'

Often during those last weeks if one of us went in the twilight to her room we would find a little silent figure sitting close beside the bed. It was Tara, or Evu, or Lullitha, three of the merriest, most healthily restless little mortals ever created. But they would sit by Ponnamal in perfect silence for an hour at a time. Others of her nurslings would come too, steal in for a kiss, and slip out again, awed by the unwonted aspect of life in that little room; but those three children minded nothing if only they might be with her. If she could bear to listen, they would tell her stories of the others, and of their gardens, and pet birds, and games; and all the old hunger of love would be in her eyes and in the tones of her voice as she listened and asked questions, drawing out their little tales. Another constant visitor was her old father, who stayed with us for months so that he might be near her. One day he asked if he might bring the barber, from time immemorial India's only physician; and finding that celebrity proposed to do no more than feel pulses, we consented, and he came.

It was a curious scene; the barber, a good friend of ours, and in his way an intelligent man, felt first the right pulse, then the left, and steadfastly regarded Ponnamal. 'How long has she to live?' demanded the old father; but this was too much for Ponnamal's sense of the ludicrous; she broke into a peal of weak laughter, and the doctor amazed turned to the father. 'There is a vitality in her,' he replied in his best medical manner, 'which it will take some weeks to reduce.' 'That is so,' murmured the old man, 'much strong food has she; milk in infinite quantities, and the essence of foods.' 'And owing to this she is as yet full of the spirit of life,' continued the doctor affably; but he stood looking at her with a puzzled expression, for she was being fed on what he regarded as nothing short of poison—rice-water for diet, with, when the pulse fails, a decoction of pig's tusk, stag's, or rhinoceros' horn, tiger's claw, and a little silver and gold, added to the ordinary medicine, being the correct treatment. Ponnamal knew this, and understanding his mind, began to tell him in Whom lay her strength and confidence and happiness; but he hardly listened. He had seen; and to that Hindu man accustomed to something very different in a sick-room, the sermon that told was written in her face.

After he left she talked of the young barber, and of her many Hindu friends in the villages about us. It appeared more than ever pitiful to her now that they should go on without the one Light which Lightens life's darkest places, slaves to the temporal, the unimportant. And a story Mr. Walker had told just before he left us seemed exactly to fit her feeling, and she longed to get all who came to see her to understand how much there was in it. It was about the carved device and inscription over three of the doors in the Milan cathedral. Over one door, roses, 'All that pleases is but for a moment,' over another a Cross, 'All that grieves us is but for a moment'; and over the central door only the words, 'Nothing is important but that which is eternal.'

Early in July we had our last sustained conversation. 'Last night,' she said, 'I had less pain than usual, and my mind was clear. When the confusion passes, and power to think returns, then my heart rises as if released from a weight; I can pray and praise. But first I examined myself to be sure all was well with me. For many days I had felt nothing, not even comfort, all was dimness and a blank and silence; then as I told my God about it He showed me that all through the days the joy of His salvation was within me, unchanged by any misery of pain. It was there, but I could not taste it. The darkness and the sadness of that time was caused by the medicine; *it was not that I had lost anything.* This comforted me, and I praised Him greatly and was content.' For many days her mouth had had that drawn look which those who have nursed anyone through sore suffering will know too well. But as she talked the old sweet, satisfied look returned, and all the old happy curves were there again. 'Oh, is it not wonderful!' she exclaimed with a sort of vigorous joyousness. 'For days and nights the waves beat hard on me, and then suddenly there is a great calm, and I lie back and rest.'

Then she asked for the last few verses of 1 Cor. 15, repeating after me the words, 'Thanks be to God which giveth us the victory.' And then I read the 46th psalm to her, and she fell asleep.

After this her words were few. Only once, as she lay in what seemed to us who were outside it unimaginable misery of body, she from the innermost core of it told me how she had hoped to be allowed to stay; she thought she could help us a little 'if the pain did not pass this limit.' It seemed to me the most unselfish word I had ever heard from human lips. And as she spoke, her eyes, the most living part of her now, seemed to devour me with the passion of love in them, and her hands held mine as if they could never let them go. Verily love is eternal: many waters cannot quench it, neither can the floods drown it; if a man would give all the substance of his house for love it would be utterly contemned.

And by this token, sure and glorious, we know the best is always in front, never behind. What can death do to that which is eternal? That which pain could not kill can death destroy? What is death but a door? They stooped as they passed through, for the door is low. Then suddenly they were unclothed and clothed upon, and clad in new garments they walked on, who shall say in what new powers of life, who shall say to what new experiences of joy? But does the dress we wear change the spirit within us? Do new powers weaken that in us which was mighty before? Do new joys blot out old loves? By all the love that ever was since love first woke in the world, it cannot be. They loved us a moment ago; with the whole strength of their being they loved us. They love us now; they will love us for ever. The old story rings true today: Those our beloved, ever beholding that Face that doth minister life to beholders, will be glad when they hear the sound of our feet stepping over our Father's threshold; for they do not forget: they love, and love cannot forget.

And so, these things being true, it must be that the best we have known is only the foretaste of some very far better to come. Can less be contained in the word that tells us we shall be satisfied with the goodness of the house? Would less than life's best content us in the land of the immortals? We shall have our best again, purified, perfected, assured from change for ever.

Thank God, there is a limit set to pain, though to love there are no limits. Ponnamal touched hers, as I have told, on August 26. It was night; but the night was full of voices, saying, 'Her warfare is accomplished': and for her it was Day.

CHAPTER 17: OUR TRIUMPHAL PROCESSION

Funeral: the word where the holy dead are concerned should be a singing word. It should shine, like a light that has suddenly broken through a rack of dark clouds. It should call with the call of bugle. We set our hearts upon causing it to be something of this for our children and the village people.

Early in the morning we filled the room with flowers. She lay as she had fallen asleep, on her little cane bed, covered with sprays of jessamine; and our friends the men servants, directed by Aruldasen whom she had loved from his childhood, carried her out, while behind her streamed the children, over a hundred of them all in white and yellow, our Dohnavur festival colours, and the little ones in blue for love. Then, valiantly led by the older girls, the children sang songs of triumph, and the one note struck, or that we tried to strike, was joy that our dear one was happy and well, with Christ; and joy, too, that we should meet her again in a little while.

There was grief, but no gloom in our hearts as we left her—not her, but the tired body that had finished its work—sown as a seed to await its resurrection. Only we wanted to follow in her steps, and run the race, and fight the fight faithful to the end. And sweet old words ran in my mind as I sought for grace to have done with selfishness: 'What a singing life is there! There is not a dumb bird in all that large field; but all sing and breathe out heaven, joy, glory, dominion to the high Prince of that new-found land.' And so, looking over 'beyond the line, and beyond death, to the laughing side of life, the world,' we did that day by the help of our God triumph and ride upon the high places of Jacob.

In the afternoon we met again in the school-room, decorated now with every joyful thing we could put in it, palms over the pictures, masses of yellow allamanda, white tuberosa growing in fragrant spikes. The room even empty looked radiant; filled as it soon was with the children in their colours, it was to me at least, like a little space of the heavenly garden let down for our comfort and gladness.

And yet it was not an easy gathering to lead into triumphant ways, for we are very human, and we wanted Ponnamal; it was difficult, most difficult, 'to learn to do without.'

We had met now to read some letters she had left for us. How well I remembered those letters being written! We were in hospital, and it was thought probable that her disease had returned, but nothing could be definitely decided without an examination under chloroform. If it proved to be cancer back again, the doctors would operate at once. The issue in that case of course must be uncertain, so that we had to go through what might be our good—bye before the operation. It was then she wrote her letters. I can see her now, sitting up in bed, eagerly and with pain—for it hurt to sit up—writing quickly. The letters finished, she asked us to sing to her; and under difficulties we sang up to the moment the stretcher-bearers came for her.

These letters were read now: there was one for the girls, and the children, the Sitties, and for me. They are, I think, too intimate for even this very intimate book. Love filled them, overflowed them; mine ended with these words: 'the kisses of eternal love.' Oh, what they miss who do not know that love is eternal!

My story has been told. It goes out into a world spent with suffering, wounded unto death. But death is not the end, it is only another beginning, and that which makes life lovable and glorious cannot die, for Love is eternal.

END

For hundreds of other excellent titles see:

www.**Classic***Christian***Ebooks**.com

Also available by Amy Carmichael:

From Sunrise Land
From the Fight
Raisins (God's Missionary)
Things As They Are
Overweights of Joy
Lotus Buds
The Continuation of a Story
Walker of Tinnevelly
Ponnamal: Her Story
From the Forest
Nor Scrip
Ragland, Spiritual Pioneer

Made in the USA
Coppell, TX
15 November 2019